Wicked
GREENVILLE

Wicked GREENVILLE

JENNIFER STOY

THE
History
PRESS

Published by The History Press
Charleston, SC
www.historypress.com

First published 2022

Manufactured in the United States

ISBN 9781467151047

Library of Congress Control Number: 2022935420

Notice: The information in this book is true and complete to the best of our knowledge. It is offered without guarantee on the part of the author or The History Press. The author and The History Press disclaim all liability in connection with the use of this book.

For John and Amelia.

CONTENTS

ACKNOWLEDGEMENTS

When I first set out to undertake this project, I wasn't sure there would be enough material to cover an entire book on true crime in Greenville. I was soon both delighted and horrified at some of the stories I found, and I am gratified to be able to expose this forgotten history to readers.

I am grateful to the staff at the Greenville County Library for always graciously setting appointments for me in the South Carolina Room during the time of COVID and scanning materials. Thanks also to Edward Blessing at the South Caroliniana Library for all the scans you generously provided. I am also indebted to the help of the Greenville Historical Society.

I have much appreciation for the friends I have made along the way in the process of publishing this book: Perry Williams, Durant Ashmore, Chad Womack and David Wall. Your love of history and storytelling helped me so much in filling in the details.

I am blessed by the encouragement of wonderful friends: Delhia Gaynor and Chip Howard; and the friends who are still with me in spirit: Jeff Welsh and Bob Pierce. I am also thankful for my parents, Priscilla and Doug (I miss you!) Saxon, who were always patient with their unusual daughter. I am also indebted to the encouragement of Cheryl Bilsland and Barbara Kakenmaster—I am so lucky to have you both in my life! I am beholden to the friendship of Charlie Porter, whose police stories planted the seed for this book many years ago.

I'd also like to give credit to Chad Rhoad and Ashley Hill at The History Press for undertaking this project and being so helpful throughout the process.

Lastly, a tremendous thank-you to my love and husband, John Stoy, who is always a sounding board for my crazy ideas and willing to go on weird field trips. He provided many of the photographs in this book, for which I am so grateful. Also, a big thanks to my daughter Amelia, who has been so patient and understanding when Mommy had to "work on the book."

1

BEGINNINGS

The city of Greenville cascades down from the Blue Ridge Mountains, a region of the Appalachians. It's a homey place that the locals call "Greenvull"; without that tell, it's difficult to discern who the natives are. Any given day on Main Street, you will see a tapestry of people, like a colorfully braided textile that could have been created in one of the mills of yesteryear. The Reedy River, its crown jewel being Falls Park, is the artery of downtown. The urban waterfall there is thirty-two feet tall, flowing from the upper Saluda River; visitors can gaze on the waters from the Liberty Bridge, held up by a framework of suspension cables. The Reedy River has long been a witness to the events of this town.

The Cherokee Natives, early settlers in this area, viewed the river as *Yunwi Gunahita*, or "Long Man," his head in the mountains and his feet in the sea. As a provider of life with water to drink, clean oneself in and grow food with, the Cherokees' ritual practice of "going to the water" was thought to wash away negativity, feelings of sadness and ailments and to restore one's soul, acting as a conduit to another world. The water spoke to them. It's no wonder that the first white settler in Greenville set up shop along this section of the Reedy River.

Greenville's utilization of its past can be seen in its cityscape, a conglomeration of cosmopolitan and traditional architecture. Old mills have been converted into luxury apartments and breweries, feed stores into trendy restaurants. Others sit empty in ruins, like dilapidated

South Main Street, circa 1918. *Courtesy of the Greenville County Library.*

mausoleums waiting to be repurposed. The Poinsett Hotel was one of the first skyscrapers of this mini metropolis, built in 1925 at twelve stories high with a distinguished opulence that remains today. One can almost hear the Count Basie Orchestra as you stroll through the lobby. The historic neighborhoods, surrounding downtown with their quaint pleasantness, also offer a window into the past, where the residents wave as you drive by.

In under an hour, you can be in Caesars Head, one of the many mountain vistas in the county with panoramic views, where an expanse of rolling green can be seen for miles and hot humid days can be escaped and replaced by a cool summer breeze. The winters are mild; a dusting of snow may stay on the ground for a week or so. This idyllic place wouldn't seem to lend itself to tales of wickedness; yet in any place humans converge, there is both beauty and ugliness. Among the dusty, long-forgotten archives, moss-covered cemeteries, hidden boxes and old newspapers, we can uncover what the Reedy knows.

WE'LL ALWAYS HAVE PEARIS

This backcountry frontier was a hostile landscape for settlers attempting to forge a life for themselves on homesteads. Vigilante citizens acted as law enforcement in the mid-1760s—an answer to a crime wave consisting of Native attacks, rogue bandits and horse thieves. These regulators regularly clashed with hunters, whom they believed "range to country with their horse and gun, without home of habitation." A lack of vagrancy laws attracted notorious vagabonds to South Carolina. Citizens petitioned British authorities for the establishment of local governments to be controlled by them as opposed to the British Crown, citing its failure in maintaining law and order.

An Anglican minister, Charles Woodmason, an early supporter and spokesman for the regulators, lamented that the hunters had no desire to be productive and that "they delight in their present low, lazy, sluttish, heathenish, hellish life" and would do anything for "liquor, cloaths [*sic*], furniture"—aside from work.

Hunters regularly angered the Cherokee by encroaching on their lands, and the settlers reaped the repercussions. Gangs of "inland bandits" frequently raided and robbed homesteads and tortured victims. Newspaper accounts told of vicious beatings, burnings, eye gougings, beehives being used as weapons and even the stealing of enslaved people. The enslaved were then used as part of the gang. Woodmason wrote that the gangs comprised "runaway negroes, free mulattoes, and other mixed blood."

In July 1769, the Circuit Court Act established a court in Ninety Six, and the regulators disbanded. Ninety Six had already been established as a settlement; Robert Goudy's trading post was there as early as 1751.

Settlers were beginning to move into the Upstate, about seventy miles north of Ninety Six. Richard Pearis is credited with being the first settler in Greenville. Born in Ireland in 1725 to George and Sarah Pearis, Pearis lived near Winchester, Virginia, with his wife, Rhoda, and three children, Richard Jr., Margaret Elizabeth and Sarah. In the mid-1750s, he was an Indian agent for Governor Robert Dinwiddie, during which time he fathered a son named George and possibly other children with a Cherokee woman. He opened a store for trade with his partner, Nathaniel Gist. Gist's father, Christopher, was one of George Washington's close friends. Washington credited him with saving his life twice in the wilderness during the French and Indian War. Pearis and the younger Gist soon fell out, but the dynamic Pearis had the trust of the Cherokee and led 130 warriors in a charge against the French at Fort Duquesne in 1758 under Major Andrew Lewis.

Pearis soon took up with Jacob Hite, a neighbor and land speculator. Together and for their own benefit, they forged a series of letters and land grants. By 1770, with a likely fraudulent deed from Cherokee leaders (either through forgery or plying them with drink), Pearis claimed land along the Reedy River, known today as Falls Park. Native interpreter John Watts wrote to Jonathan Stuart, superintendent of Indian Affairs in May 1770, that Pearis was "a very dangerous fellow who will breed great disturbances if he is let alone" and went on to charge that Pearis would tell the Natives lies to curry favor with them. A 1739 South Carolina law prohibited Natives from selling lands to non-Natives, but with undetermined boundaries, there was not much that could be done by royal officials. In 1772, a provincial boundary was established, and Stuart went to Charleston (then Charles Town) to report to Governor Charles Montagu that Pearis and Hite had either forged or coerced land grants and should be prosecuted. Pearis and Hite were tried at the settlement of Ninety Six in 1773. Pearis relinquished his deed but quicky regained it by having it signed over to him by his half-Cherokee son. Pearis schemed to do this with more parcels, growing his holdings and selling land to others, including Hite. Stuart wrote to the Cherokee in 1775, complaining that they were "constantly listening to Richard Pearis, who cheats you of your lands."

Greenville was located at a middle point between settlements in the areas of Ninety Six and present-day Spartanburg. By the time the Battles of Lexington and Concord set off the Revolutionary War in April 1775, lines were being drawn in the backcountry of South Carolina. Charismatic brothers Robert and Patrick Cunningham were early organizers of large groups of Loyalists in and around the settlement at Ninety Six. In early June 1775, the provincial congress of South Carolina established the Council of Safety and established a "rebel government" body. William Henry Drayton, a lawyer and planter born and raised at Drayton Hall in Charleston, was selected to travel to the upcountry to rally support for the Patriot cause and help ease concerns over the British-sympathizing Cherokee.

Pearis had gained notoriety for being potentially dangerous to the Patriots and was deemed someone who should be watched. Despite this, Drayton took him along as a mediator at a meeting with Cherokee leaders in September 1775. Until this time, the British had been supplying the Cherokee with goods, including gunpowder and lead for their hunting seasons, which Pearis charitably volunteered to distribute. Drayton promised that the Patriots would

Falls at the Reedy River, where Richard Pearis made his home. *Photograph by John Stoy.*

take over this role in exchange for their support. Ever in self-preservation mode, Pearis had orchestrated this meeting with the pretext that the Council of Safety would name him superintendent of Indian Affairs, and when that did not pan out, his loyalty to the British was solidified.

Shortly after Pearis and Drayton held court with the Cherokee, Drayton deemed Robert Cunningham too dangerous to be at large, and he was arrested and sent to jail in Charleston. Patrick Cunningham was infuriated by this and organized a posse of about sixty men to free his brother. Pearis convinced him that a wagon train of munitions was being sent to the Cherokee by the Patriots for use against Cunningham and his merry band of king's men. Cunningham and his men, unsuccessful in freeing Robert, succeeded in overwhelming the guards and absconding with the wagon of gunpowder and lead. On November 8, Drayton penned a letter to Pearis from Charleston, advising him that Colonel Richard Richardson and his rangers had been charged by Congress to apprehend those involved "in this daring act." He further asked if Pearis would be so good as to make this known to Cunningham and his men and to make it known to the Natives "that they may at once see that the head men of South Carolina are faithful to their engagements, & that they will not suffer their lawful authority to be trampled upon with impunity." On November 11, in an affidavit sworn to in Ninety Six, Pearis attempted to slander Drayton's character and attested that Drayton had promised him a commission after setting up the meeting, that he was coercing the Natives to "fight against the White man for the committee" and that Drayton had further promised to settle a "personal debt" for him, which he had not done. He further claimed that after receiving Drayton's reprimand, the ammunition was forwarded to the Natives three days before he arrived in Ninety Six, and that was also when he learned that Robert Cunningham had been taken "prisoner by some of the committee party." He had a way of talking his way out of things.

Colonel Andrew Williamson marched to Ninety Six with a militia, intending to regain the munitions, but Pearis and Cunningham were ready. Williamson's men constructed a crude, makeshift fort but were outnumbered by Loyalists. The two sides traded volleys for a few days before ultimately agreeing to a truce. After receiving word of this confrontation, Colonel Richardson readied his regiment of about 1,000 men and alerted the council that the Loyalists were feeling emboldened by their skirmish at Ninety Six and that his men were ready to put them down. Richardson soon joined forces with the new Spartan Regiment, led by Colonel John Thomas, along with other companies, increasing Richardson's command to about 2,500 men. On December 8, he issued a declaration in which he named Patrick Cunningham and others for committing an act of "dangerous insurrection and commotion" and further accused them of "robbery, murder and breach of peace." He stated that the men had to be delivered up within five days or he would be forced to take "such steps as will be found disagreeable" but which were for the "public good." Several Loyalists gave up their guns, but none of the leaders surrendered. Governor William Campbell of the provincial assembly was living in fear and exile aboard the Royal Navy's HMS *Tamar* in Charleston Harbor. On December 12, with regimental numbers then nearing about 3,000, Richardson took several prisoners, including Richard Pearis. The insurgents were sent to Charleston while Richardson sent Thompson and about 1,300 militiamen up the Reedy River, where, at dawn on December 22, 1775, they took Cunningham's men by surprise and regained the munitions. Cunningham escaped on horseback while shouting for every man to "shift for himself!"

Location of the Battle of Great Cane Brake. *Photograph by John Stoy.*

The Battle of Great Cane Brake was the only Revolutionary War battle fought in Greenville County. While gunpowder scented the frigid air, at least 5 Loyalists were dead, and the Patriots took 130 prisoners. Thompson reunited with Richardson's camp through an unusually heavy snowstorm. Those tentless, poorly dressed and frostbitten but victorious men are remembered today as the men of the "Snow Campaign."

While Pearis languished in chains like a buried and forgotten chest in Charleston, tensions were high on the southern frontier. Distrust grew among Loyalists and "rebels," continued "land encroachment" angered the Cherokee and Native raids were commonplace. Settlers hid out in nearby forts designed for this purpose.

With the government then forced to act in dealing with the "Indian problem," Pearis used his eloquent words to petition the council to help fight the Cherokee, putting their differences aside to combat a common enemy. This seemed reasonable to the council, and it released both Pearis and Robert Cunningham. Cunningham and Pearis reported to Colonel Williamson to join up with the Patriots, but Williamson was leery and did not sign them.

Pearis returned to Greenville to find that his home was "burnt and destroyed" and his wife and children run out of town by Colonel John Thomas. Pearis soon reunited with his family and went to Charleston, where he bewitched Governor John Rutledge and was promised protection. He then appealed to the state legislature to return his stolen enslaved people and livestock and to provide compensation for his destroyed property. But he was deemed an "enemy of the state," and the men responsible for the destruction, namely Ezekiel Polk, under orders from Williamson, were granted immunity. Pearis was on shifting sand and hightailed it to Florida in 1777, eventually arriving on foot in Pensacola, where he commanded two small companies for the British.

Sir Henry Clinton called on Pearis to travel to the backcountry of South Carolina to inform the Loyalists to ready themselves for the imminent arrival of British troops. The British orders instructed Pearis to "seize and secure such of the people as have been most subservient to the purposes of the rebellious leaders" but not to conduct "any doubtful, offensive operations." Robert Cunningham had already organized a large Loyalist following, and the required guerrilla tactics were right up Pearis's alley. Pearis was reported to have at least six thousand men; it was also reported that rebel forts were destroyed and that he "imprisoned their leaders to the numbers of forty."

Clinton, comfortable with his support in the backcountry, left Charles Cornwallis and his commanders in charge. However, Cornwallis did not hold Pearis or his tactics in high regard, and soon, he released the rebel leaders and returned their arms. A deflated Pearis must have felt that all his accomplishments had been undone and his valor marginalized. Lieutenant Colonel Balfour wrote to Cornwallis that the "infamous character" Pearis should be sent home before he caused further "distress amongst the inhabitants." It could be theorized that this series of missteps on the part of the British led to the victories at Cowpens and Kings Mountain.

Pearis was eventually recaptured by American forces while ironically defending Fort Cornwallis in Augusta, Georgia, in June 1781.

After he was paroled, Pearis returned to Florida and eventually ended up in the Bahamas, a popular destination for many Loyalists after the war. He wrote to the commissioners appointed by acts of Parliament, lamenting the destruction of his Greenville property and explaining what his family had been through:

> *In the year 1776, when my estate was burnt and destroyed, my wife, two daughters and one son were surprised by break of day by one Colonel Thomas and 400 militia; beat and abused my daughters and made them all prisoners after burning, destroying and carrying away the property, forced them to march thro' [sic] rivers and creeks on foot 25 miles in one*

day, without victuals or any thing [sic] *to cover their heads from the sun; afterwards, kept them confined three days without any provisions, then sent them off in an open wagon 100 miles and turned them out to shift for themselves amongst a parcel of rebels without money or provisions. They were then obliged for three years during my absences on duty to be depending on charitable people added to their own industry for their living and under continual apprehension of being massacred.*

He ultimately received compensation for his destroyed property, as well as a British pension until he died in 1794. He bequeathed several acres of land in the West Indies to his wife and children. George, his Cherokee son, who, by all accounts, remained in America, was left out of his will.

Richard Pearis Jr. married Margaret Cunningham, the daughter of Robert Cunningham, who also moved to the Bahamas after the Revolution.

Patrick Cunningham remained in South Carolina and was even elected to the legislature. His granddaughter Ann Pamela Cunningham was instrumental in the saving and restoration of Washington's Mount Vernon. She was the founder of the Mount Vernon Ladies' Association in 1853.

Today, Paris Mountain, named for Richard Pearis, located on land that he once owned, stands as a testament to a maverick who lived by his wits, with cunning skills for survival and self-preservation, in the savage backcountry.* Though he is often described as a scoundrel, his exploits laid the foundations for Greenville's existence, paving the way for the next wave of pioneers.

THE "INDIAN PROBLEM"

Backcountry citizens on both sides of the Revolution distrusted each other and the Cherokee. Life among the Indians was sometimes harmonious, and other times, it was not. The "nots" were brutal and savage. Settlement attacks were met with reprisals, and a vicious cycle would ensue. Stockade forts were built and used to shelter families from Native raids. Local folklore tells of Mrs. Thompson, who took shelter in Woods Fort, near the Greenville/Spartanburg County line, with what must have been a massive

---

* The genealogist in me feels compelled to explain that standard spellings of last names weren't really thought of as important until the 1850s. Phonetic spellings were common, as seen in records regarding Richard Pearis/Paris—thus the spelling of Paris Mountain.

headache, as she had been scalped; yet somehow, she managed to recover from her wounds. In July 1775, Robert Goudy of the Ninety Six trading post swore in an affidavit that he had received intelligence from "a certain Cherokee Indian named the 'Man Killer of Keowee'" that the British were "encouraging the Cherokees to fall upon the White people in South Carolina" and that they had been given "presents of rum" by British Indian agent Alexander Cameron. In May 1776, Cameron persuaded the Cherokee to believe that Patriot forces were planning an attack on them and captured Indian traders Preston and Edward Hampton, forcing an oath of neutrality in exchange for their release. James Hite, the son of Jacob, attempted to capture Cameron and was scalped and killed. Notwithstanding his former associations with the Cherokee, Jacob Hite and the rest of his family soon suffered the same bloody fate. A barbarous extermination took place in July 1776, when the family of Anthony Hampton, the father of Preston and Edward, was massacred. Preston was aware that the Cherokee were on the warpath and had come home to warn his family. Anthony; his wife, Elizabeth; eight-year-old John Bynum (Anthony's grandson); and the infant of Elizabeth and James Harrison (Anthony and Elizabeth's daughter and son-in-law) were also in the house situated along the Tiger River. No sooner had Preston arrived with his warning than the Cherokee were at the door. Anthony Hampton extended his hand in a friendly handshake. In that moment, he watched in horror as Preston was shot and struck dead. The warrior shaking Anthony's hand immediately sank a tomahawk into his head, splitting it like soft firewood. Anthony's wife, Elizabeth, was likely scalped, left butchered with her innards exposed. Elizabeth Harrison's baby was repeatedly bashed against a wall, sending blood and brain matter flying with each deathblow. Inexplicably, the Cherokee took eight-year-old John Bynum with them before burning the Hampton homestead to the ground. The charred remains were then hastily interred on the property, and last rites were performed by neighbors.

In retaliation, Captain Thomas Howard, a scout who had settled on land in the Tigerville area, gathered up some raiders, determined to put an end to these uprisings. Howard was led by a Cherokee guide named Skyuka, whom tradition says was indebted to Howard for nursing him back to health after a rattlesnake bite. In the moonlight, Skyuka convoyed Howard's party through a secret trail up Round Mountain and, coming up from the rear, executed nearly all the gathered Natives. Skyuka was deemed an enemy to the Cherokee, with one tale suggesting the Native had his tongue cut out while he was drawn and quartered on White Oak Mountain. Another says

Above: Hampton homestead area. *Photograph by John Stoy.*

Left: Hampton Monument. *Photograph by John Stoy.*

that he was eventually caught by Loyalists and hanged from a tree on what is today referred to as Skyuka Creek.

John Bynum, the little boy captured by Natives in the Hampton Massacre, was released in 1777, after a treaty was signed that ceded lands to white settlers. Bynum family lore tells us that he was ransomed by his uncle Wade Hampton I, and he left his Native "family" reluctantly. Bynum later became a surveyor for South Carolina and died in 1822 in Columbia at the age of fifty-four, having never spoken publicly about the carnage he witnessed the day of the massacre. The earliest published account of the fatalities was written by George Howe in *History of the Presbyterian Church* in 1870. In John Landrum's book *Colonial Revolutionary History of Upper South Carolina*, published in 1897, he references a letter from Professor Wm. S. Morrison, who describes the location of the graves confirmed by neighbors. It is possible that the graves were known to locals for some time, possibly up until the 1930s, but they were eventually lost with the expansion of the area, including the construction of Wade Hampton Boulevard (Highway 29). In 1933, a monument was erected near the site by the United Daughters of the Confederacy; the marker has since been moved closer to the road, as the site is currently used as commercial property.

A large obelisk presently stands at Stearns Park in Columbus, North Carolina, commemorating the Battle of Round Mountain and paying tribute to Thomas Howard and his trusty guide, Skyuka.

A MOTLEY CREW

Undeterred by the surrender of the British at Yorktown in October, terror was still reigning in the backwoods. A raid on Gowen's Fort by William "Bloody Bill" Bates took place in November. With a force of Loyalists and Natives, he tortured and killed men "on the spot." No military records for Bates have ever been found, suggesting that he was nothing more than a bandit, looting and pillaging indiscriminately. A man named John Motley (whose parents had been butchered by Bates) had been singled out for torture but managed to escape. According to an account later written by South Carolina governor Benjamin F. Perry, Bates was arrested several years after the war for stealing a horse and jailed in Greenville. Motley gathered a small mob and, in a classic example of vigilante justice, remanded the keys from the sheriff and jailer, Colonel Carter, at gunpoint. Carter urged Motley to "let the law take its course," noting that "the wretch will meet his doom on the gallows." "No," Motley replied, determined to avenge his family, "talk not to me of the slow and uncertain process of the law; the blood of my murdered father and mother cries to me for revenge, and I will have it—the gallows will not rob me of my victim—hesitate another moment at the peril of your own life." Carter saw madness in Motley's eyes and handed him the keys without a fight. Motley dragged Bates outside, allegedly shouting, "Die scoundrel, and receive the punishment your hellish life has merited," before he shot him in the street. Perry reported that he "fell without uttering a syllable, and was buried where he fell, at the prison door," at the modern-day corner of South Main and West Broad Streets. Motley returned the keys and rode on home. He never faced prosecution. Perhaps revenge is a dish best served in broad daylight on a busy street.

THE GOOD SHERIFF

A race to invest in real estate and develop the Greenville area created a rivalry between Lemuel J. Alston and Elias Earle. In 1786, Alston purchased over eleven thousand acres, including lands once owned by Richard Pearis. The extensive holdings became known as "Alston's Plat," tracts that were planned for resale, becoming the nexus of a downtown area called Pleasantburg. In 1787, Earle began to accrue land just north of Alston's tracts. Within a few years, the locals demanded a centralized courthouse. Petitions from Alston and Earle to build the courthouse on their lands were won by Alston. With the courthouse completed, Alston's land became a city center, with stores and a post office soon going up. Overlooking the Reedy River, Alston built a mansion called Prospect Hill and started a flour mill and foundry. Earle operated a foundry on the Saluda River and represented Congress in the Eighth Congressional District.

A judicial district was formed called the Washington District, and it covered the counties of present-day Greenville, Anderson and Pickens. In 1795, a local Revolutionary War hero, Robert Maxwell, was appointed as the first official sheriff.

Captain Maxwell, as he was known, was a neighbor and friend of a man named Dr. Joshua Kennedy. Both were known as southern gentlemen in high society and were well liked in the community. The two men apparently had a falling out over the trivial matter of a watch taken in error by Maxwell

Main Street, showing the old courthouse to the left. *Courtesy of the Greenville County Library.*

during some travels, thinking it was his own. With the misunderstanding rectified, Kennedy continued to spread gossip of this incident to whoever would listen. Maxwell took this as a personal insult and accused Kennedy of repeated slander; a bitter rift flared up.

In November 1797, Maxwell was on his way to court when he was ambushed and shot several times. He lost three fingers on his left hand and was hit in his side, legs and thighs. Remarkably, Maxwell rode home, but he was in sorry shape. Earlier that same day, Maxwell's barn had been set on fire but was quickly extinguished. Maxwell lingered for a couple of days but ultimately succumbed to his injuries. His murder is considered the first casualty of the Greenville County Sheriff's Office.

Maxwell's friends were greatly agitated and demanded the immediate arrest of Dr. Kennedy, whom they deemed very suspicious, but Kennedy had an alibi. He had been living in Georgia for several months. Maxwell's friends decided to usurp the law and employed two men, a detective named General Blair and a very large man named Ben Starrett, to go get Kennedy and bring him to Greenville for trial.

Blair and Starrett traveled to a village in Georgia, stopping at a hotel for the night. Blair feigned illness so that the doctor could be called. Dr. Kennedy arrived to tend to the patient and was captured. They roughed him up a bit and rode back to face the court.

Court records reveal that Dr. Kennedy supplied rifles to his brother William Ebenezer Kennedy and a "mulatto man called Tom" and, with "malice aforethought," conspired to "kill and murder" Robert Maxwell. Tom had apparently been promised freedom in exchange for setting Maxwell's barn ablaze and shooting him. Jurors essentially reasoned that the "Devil made him do it," and the brothers Kennedy were found not guilty. Newspapers reported that the "negro was sentenced to death," so Tom was apparently not as lucky.

END-OF-CENTURY CRIMES

The close of the century saw the population of Greenville continue to grow. With the advancement of a "wagon road," drovers were able to bring in livestock. With the drovers came camps, and with the camps came taverns, gambling, prostitution and liquor. Most crimes comprised your run-of-the-mill horse stealing, larceny, counterfeiting and selling spiritous liquors, but the occasional misdeed would send a shockwave through the burgeoning town. Such was the 1794 case of Samuel Owens, who was accused of "buggery" for having carnal knowledge of a mare; or James Bell, who bit off the nose of Terry Tarrant without "sufficient provocation." The jury found him guilty, but he broke out of jail. A note in the court file stated "non est inventus"—in other words, he couldn't be found. A gloomy case was the 1798 rape of Amy Ivy by Burrell Green. He pushed his way through her door, forced her into bed and "took his will of her." The jury found him not guilty, as he was "moved and seduced by the instigation of the Devil"—so it went on the frontier.

2

ANTEBELLUM ANTICS

*A*ntebellum Greenville was the antithesis of the rest of the South. Cotton was not cultivated in abundance, and while the upper-class gentry relied on the labor of the enslaved, slavery was not common among the majority of working-class folk. There was a population of free Black people, who had been freed after the Revolutionary War, and the district was resolutely Unionist.

The South Carolina Canal and Railroad Company was established in 1827 to build a line from Charleston to Hamburg, thus increasing the ease of getting goods and crops between the Lowcountry and Upstate. Greenville industrialist Vardry McBee oversaw the completion of a depot between Pendleton and Augusta Streets. McBee was also instrumental in the expansion of schools and churches in the area.

DEAR THEODOSIA

As 1812 approached, Greenvillians worried about becoming embroiled in an impending war, but local men signed up for the militias in large numbers. Outbreaks of malaria, mostly in the Lowcountry, terrified people, and overall enlistment for the militia in the state was low. Men were more concerned about contracting "country fever" than being harmed in battle, much to the dismay of then-governor Joseph Alston (no relation to Lemuel). Alston was one of many people of influence who built a summer home on Alice Street in Greenville, as it gained a reputation as a resort destination.

The second war of American independence was fought on land and sea against the British forces, along with their Native and Canadian allies. Amid the Napoleonic Wars, Britain took to the practice of impressment, in which they, like pirates, took men from American ships and forced them into service in the Royal Navy. The French and British placed trade sanctions on the young country, sending the United States into a crippling depression. President Madison and Congress declared war on the British, beginning with an attack on Canada with the objective of gaining land and putting a damper on British supply lines to the Native confederation in the northwest. William Henry Harrison's forces did manage to kill Native leader Tecumseh, but the American troops were greatly outnumbered and inexperienced.

Alston was the governor of South Carolina from 1812 to 1814. His wife, Theodosia Burr, was the daughter of Aaron Burr—yes, that Aaron Burr—Jefferson's vice president who infamously shot and killed Alexander Hamilton in a duel in 1804. Born into the lap of luxury, Theodosia's life was tragic and filled with great sorrow. The financially troubled Burr most likely played matchmaker when encouraging the relationship between his educated daughter and Alston. Alston was a wealthy rice planter, well-connected in southern politics. They married in 1801 and are thought to

Where Theodosia Burr once resided in Greenville. *Courtesy of the South Caroliniana Library, University of South Carolina, Columbia, SC.*

Left: Nags Head portrait. *Courtesy of the Lewis Walpole Library, Yale University.*

Right: Theodosia Burr (Mrs. Joseph Alston). *Courtesy of the Yale University Art Gallery.*

have been the first couple to ever honeymoon at Niagara Falls. Theodosia had a very difficult pregnancy that produced a son, Aaron Burr Alston, in 1802. Healthwise, she never quite recovered from this and continued to struggle with bouts of illness. She was very close to her father, who, after the duel, his political career in ruins, moved to Europe in a self-imposed exile. This caused great stress for Theodosia. To make matters worse, her ten-year-old son—her only son—succumbed to malaria in 1812. Theodosia and Alston were both deeply melancholic. Burr eventually made his return to New York, and Alston arranged for his wife to set sail on a ship called the *Patriot* to be reunited with her father. Alston remained in South Carolina as head of the dwindling militia but wrote a letter to the British government to allow safe passage for his wife, as warships patrolled the Atlantic Coast. Burr sent an associate, Dr. Timothy Greene, to accompany Theodosia. On December 31, 1812, the ship set sail from Georgetown, and then—nothing. Theodosia and the passengers of the schooner were never heard from again. They were lost at sea, under the zodiac.[*]

---

[*] The phrase "to the zodiac" appears in the poem "Kitty Hawk" by Robert Frost, which was inspired by the story of Theodosia Burr Alston.

A sorrowful Alston corresponded regularly with Burr. Both men were frantic for any news about the fate of their beloved Theodosia. A severe storm off Cape Hatteras the night the ship departed is the likely answer; however, speculation continues today. Deathbed confessions over the years of old pirates and plunderers have added to the mystery.

On December 24, 1824, the Treaty of Ghent ended the War of 1812 without the loss or gain of any territory for the United States, and relations between America and Britain were basically restored.

A portrait surfaced in 1869, when it was given as payment to a physician in Nags Head, with a story that it had come from the spoils of a sunken ship during the War of 1812. The doctor was convinced it was Theodosia, even though family members could never quite confirm it was her. Over two hundred years later, Theodosia's fate and the "Nags Head portrait" remain unsolved questions. A broken-hearted Joseph Alston died in 1816 at the age of thirty-seven from possible complications of malaria.

REBELLION BREWING

"Political theatrics" entertained the citizenry of Greenville in 1806 with a heated election for the congressional seat of Elias Earle. Lemuel Alston and another member of the local gentry, Dr. William Hunter, got into the three-way race, which seemed to be determined by who could supply the most whiskey on the stump. This popularity contest was ultimately won by Alston. Greenville was staunchly Unionist, and unlike the Lowcountry, it was not a plantation society. Few had enslaved people. As early as 1797, clergy began to make some nervous, as they asked if slavery was "agreeable to the gospel." The early 1820s saw the publishing of pamphlets that encouraged emancipation, and the legislature tried to curtail the flow of enslaved people from the North to South Carolina. Wealthy plantation owners were juxtaposed against large numbers of freed Black people working as merchants and contractors, and pressure was building. In 1822, a freed Black man living in Charleston named Denmark Vesey planned an insurrection with an army of enslaved people. He began holding secret meetings and collecting weapons. Vesey intended to take over the United States Arsenal in Charleston, burn the city and murder the governor, along with white people and any Black people who did not join their fight—he even ordered his brigade to not spare any women or children. The plot was uncovered and abated, but by then, the state was terrified. Newspapers would barely report or discuss the escalating power of abolitionists, as it was deemed too dangerous. Grumblings of states' rights began brewing in South Carolina.

The enslaved continued to suffer. In July 1851, an enslaved woman was killed in such a brutal fashion that her brain was described as mostly "in a fluid condition." The poor woman's name is lost to history, and she is listed in court documents as "negro woman slave." Westly Pattison, the brother of her owner, William Pattison, had whipped her so heinously that it killed her—her humanity diminished with every blow. Pattison stated that he gave her two hundred lashes but that he had seen her complaining later that night. By the time her body was found, the state of decomposition was so bad that it was impossible to identify where her injuries were. Jurors reasoned that they couldn't determine that she had come to her death by whipping. In August 1851, Mose, a man owned by George French, was found hanging from a tree by a hemp cord. Court documents report that Mose didn't have "God before his eyes" and was "a felon of himself" who, "voluntarily and of his malice aforethought, himself killed, strangled and murdered against the peace of this state." Things also did not go well for a man named Allen in 1858. He shot himself in the forehead with a rifle to avoid a whipping; he borrowed the rifle on the pretext of shooting some squirrels. He had been overheard saying that he would "slit his throat" before ever being whipped again. Strongly spiritual, the numbers of enslaved who committed suicide were relatively low, consistent with people of African descent in Africa and other parts of the world. But heinous conditions led to the unthinkable.

While the abolitionist movement was gaining converts, many South Carolinians perceived slavery as a constitutional right, falling under property rights. Growing calls for secession started to take root, but proslavery Unionists did not want to give up their country. Abolitionists met in secret. Distrust among neighbors, reminiscent of the distrust between rebels and Loyalists, was starting to fester. In December 1851, a successful Greenville tea maker, Junius Smith, was beaten severely at his home by a slave patrol, because he was merely suspected of favoring abolition. Newspapers compared the incident to the Spanish Inquisition. The *Southern Patriot* told its readers, "Southern people will defend the institution of African slavery at all hazards, the last extremity. [But the radical secessionists] would weaken & destroy the institution of slavery & involve the country in civil war & ruinous taxation." It appeared there could be no compromise.

FATAL WORDS

In the early 1830s, the Nullification Crisis was heating up. Vice president and South Carolinian John C. Calhoun believed that the states had a right to ignore (or nullify) any laws the state deemed to be unconstitutional, namely recent tariff laws that affected trade in South Carolina.

Lawyer Benjamin Franklin Perry began his foray into politics in 1832, when he was at the helm of the Unionist newspaper the *Greenville Mountaineer* at the height of the nullification process—to the great ire of other South Carolina politicians, especially Calhoun. Calhoun's acolytes, namely Greenvillian legislator Waddy Thompson (a vehement supporter of Calhoun's), had duped Turner Bynum, a handsome, young, ambitious man from Columbia, to come to Greenville and start a rival paper, the *Sentinel*. Bynum published an attack on Perry, comparing him to the serpent that "wooed Eve to commit sin by a tempting lie." With Perry's honor called into question, he had no choice but to do what any southern gentleman would do at the time: challenge Bynum to a duel. The trap had been set. Hothead Perry had already been in at least a dozen physical fights over his political beliefs, nearly coming to blows with Thompson on more than one occasion. The nullifiers were confident Perry would be destroyed, either by cowardice of not following through or ending up dead—either way, they would be rid of him and his influential editorials. Bynum was known as an excellent shot. Perry wrote in his diary that Bynum and the *Sentinel* were brought to Greenville by Thompson, who "made a tool of Bynum to destroy me."

Like the arena deaths of antiquity, dueling was, as described by Random House, "a prearranged combat between two persons, fought with deadly weapons, according to an accepted code of procedure" and was seen as a sanctioned way of handling disagreements. Dueling was a southern pastime and was reported in the newspapers like baseball stats. As described in the *People's Journal* of Pickens, the rules "of the code of duello always possess a charm, the more especially if the parties to it are prominent and results tragic."

Perry confided in his diary that Thompson and the nullifiers had "made unreal attempts to black my reputation and take my life." He waxed poetic that "life is not of much consequence to me, but the grief and distress it will cause my parents that any misfortune befall me." He even penned a statement "to the people of Greenville," in which he stated that he was indebted to them for letting him be a public servant and that if he is killed by the editor of the *Sentinel* that "they" have accomplished their goal in getting rid of him.

Above: Island at Hatton's Ford on Tugaloo River, near where the Perry/Bynum duel took place. *Photograph by John Stoy.*

Left: The grave of Turner Bynum at the Old Stone Church Cemetery. *Photograph by John Stoy.*

He called out Waddy Thompson for being the "behind the curtain, principle [*sic*] actor in the tragedy. He brought Bynum to this place."

At sunrise on the morning of August 16, 1832, Perry and Bynum met on an island at Hatton's Ford, near the Tugaloo River. Afterward, Perry noted that Bynum "looked unusually pale." After the customary fifteen paces, Bynum fired instantly, grazing Perry. Perry's bullet hit Bynum in the stomach and took off the tip of his finger. Perry wore a coat with a red lining, which the surgeon mistook for blood, and he tore the coat open to reveal that Perry was unharmed. Perry rushed to Bynum and spoke to him, saying, "I hope, sir, you are not mortally hurt," to which Bynum replied, "I would hate to die of so trifling a wound; I hope to live to renew the fight."

Bynum died a few hours later and was buried by friends outside the graveyard wall of Old Stone Church in Pendleton in the middle of the night in the pouring rain. He was twenty-eight. Apparently, one could not be killed in a duel and buried in a churchyard. Neighborhood lore, retold many times over, stated that there were two trees marking Bynum's grave that were referred to as the "dueling trees." The trees eventually died, and the graveyard expanded, enclosing the grave within it.

Perry wrote in his diary, "Bynum was buried on Saturday night, and my feelings are bad." He thanked God for his mercy and recounted, "On my return from the place, I met Bynum's brother. We shook hands and had a long talk. He told me that there was nothing of ill will in his feeling towards me."

Perry feared Thompson and the nullifiers would continue their vendetta and stated in the *Mountaineer* that his dueling days with rival editors were finished. He wrote that if he chose to duel again, it "shall be a man of distinction. I am done with lackeys." The *Sentinel* lasted six months before shuttering its doors for the last time, as Union sentiment in Greenville was at an all-time high. Malinda McBee, the daughter of "father of Greenville" Vardry McBee, was so besotted with Bynum that she never married and even "covenanted never again to look at herself in a mirror." She lived until 1890, when she died at the age of eighty-two. Perry eventually became the seventy-second governor of South Carolina, and in his later years, he acknowledged that the duel was a very "painful event" and one of the "dark spots" of his life.

Another southern gentleman who brought himself some trouble over honor was William Lowndes Yancey. Yancey had also been the editor of the *Greenville Mountaineer* and was very vocal about his anti-Calhoun stance. In fact, you could say it was his mouth that got him into this trouble. He was overheard making a disparaging political remark at a debate that featured congressional candidates Waddy Thompson and Joseph Witner.

Above: Mansion House. *Courtesy of the Greenville County Library.*

Left: William Lowndes Yancey. *Courtesy of the Greenville County Library.*

He called Thompson a scoundrel and was confronted by seventeen-year-old Elias Earle. Earle was Thompson's nephew and a cousin of Yancey's wife, Sarah Earle Yancey. Yancey slapped the young Earle to "chastise his insolence"; Earle called him a "damned liar" and hit him with a riding crop. The altercation was broken up, and Yancey met with Earle's father, Dr. Robinson Earle, the next day to try to explain the events that had taken place, but neither Earle was satisfied. On September 8, 1838, Yancey and Dr. Earle had a confrontation on Main Street in front of the Mansion House (near the present-day Westin Poinsett Hotel). Earle again called Yancey "a damned liar," to which Yancey responded in turn by drawing his pistol and shooting the sixty-two-year-old Earle. Yancey proceeded to beat him with the butt of his gun in broad daylight. He also drew a sword and attempted to stab the dying doctor but was pulled away from the fight.

Yancey was taken to the jail in Greenville and wrote to his brother that he had secured "a legacy" for his son, as people would know better than to besmirch a Yancey. Dueling aficionado Benjamin Perry acted as one of Yancey's lawyers. The jury decided Yancey was guilty of manslaughter. He was sentenced to serve a year in jail and pay a fine of $1,500, but his sentence was commuted by Governor Patrick Noble. Yancey went on to have a political career.

Perhaps there was something in the water at the offices of the *Greenville Mountaineer*, because in 1845, Dexter Wells, an office boy and nephew of then-editor O.H. Wells, shot Robert Headden in cold blood. One newspaper account reported that Wells had been lying in wait with a two-year-old grudge against Headden, even though they hadn't spoken in years. "Seduction and Murder" was the headline of another newspaper account, which proclaimed that Headden had seduced Well's sister, writing that it "comes as near justifiable homicide as any murder can." Headden remained in agony for over twenty-four hours before succumbing to his wounds. Wells must have been light in the political connections, because he was given a "necktie sociable" and hanged.

SPIRITS, LAUDANUM AND AN AXE

The people of Greenville were tickled when Chang and Eng Bunker visited the city in 1834. The "Siamese twins" enthralled audiences with their sideshow entertainment. The *Charleston Courier*, on December 15, 1834, described the conjoined men as "highly interesting in their appearance." Other entertainers graced the city at this time, including the Greenville Brass Band and touring musical and dramatic acts. The use of intoxicants for personal entertainment was also on the rise.

Aside from alcohol, laudanum (an opium derivative) was the drug of choice in the 1800s. Used regularly by respected doctors and quacks alike, it "cured" everything, from gunshot wounds, headaches and stomach pains to menstrual cramps and "diseases of a nervous character." Laudanum was given to Alexander Hamilton to comfort him as he died from wounds he received in his duel with Aaron Burr. This medicine cured little but offered a dream-like state that was highly addictive, and many people met their ends due to its effects. Such was the case of Samuel W. Bates, who, by all accounts, overdosed at McBride's Hotel in July 1851.

Bates had once been a successful landowner in Christ Church Parish (present-day Mount Pleasant), and according to the 1830 census, he had a wife and family, but by 1850, he was alone and working as a carpenter. The inquest into his death revealed that he had squandered away any fortune he had, and at almost sixty years old, he had no place to live. Bates arrived in Greenville via the Columbia Stage on June 28, 1851, coming to town presumably to meet an old acquaintance named George Dyer.

Dyer testified that he had known Bates for thirty years but had not seen him in ten and did not believe that he had any fixed residence. He described Bates as a "dissipated man." Other witnesses alleged that Bates had complained of stomach pains and purchased the laudanum, which he took and then protested that it was no good, even demanding his money back, which he did not get. Bates asked for a physician to be sent for and languished in agony for several hours, eventually dying of a combination of alcohol and laudanum poisoning, per the doctor.

February 1856 saw some excitement in the Chick Springs area of Taylors when Gipson Southern was murdered by a man named Bruce with an axe to the spine. A "jug of mean liquor and two equally as mean women" were also blamed in an account reported in the *Greenville Enterprise* newspaper.

The *Greenville Enterprise* also reported the sad tale of John Prince, twenty-nine, who was found dead from intoxication in July 1856, a love of whiskey being the undoing of this young barkeep. Prince pawned his own coat for a little "nerve tonic." The paper implored Greenville citizens to "throw themselves in the way of this great evil" and pleaded for temperance. It wondered how long the community would suffer while sharing the same black-and-white page with a recipe for blackberry wine.

Perhaps still in a Christmas mood, Elijah Pike dropped dead from "excessive use of ardent spirits" on December 28, 1856, leaving behind five children. Pike had seemed lively early in the day. But he soon took to bed, complaining of stomach pains. A lodger, Mr. Charles Wynn, stated at the coroner's inquest that Pike had been drinking heavily for several months. He thought Pike was asleep and went out to enjoy the season for a while before returning to find Pike had gone into "that good night."*

---

* "Do not go gentle into that good night." Dylan Thomas, *Selected Poems* (London: Orion Publishing Group, 1934), 80.

3

MOONSHINE AND MAYHEM

*I*f Greenville is the "Wild West" of the Blue Ridge, Dark Corner was its Deadwood. This isolated and infamous section of the county near Glassy Mountain was once the home of outlaws, gunfighters, vengeance-seekers and moonshiners.

The legend says that at the height of the nullification crisis, a politician was preaching to a group in the area when the pro-Union crowd overturned his cart. The man accused them of "living in the dark," and the area's moniker was born.

The mountain folk whose roots stretched back to the Revolution and Cherokee wars were not interested in serving the Confederacy and fighting in the "rich man's war," and those who did likely did not return at all or came home crippled or maimed. Natural springs, hidden "hollers" and ample corn fields made Dark Corner a perfect place to make "likker." The *Greenville News* reported that it was hard to find a clean drink of water in the area, as the streams were contaminated with "distillery waste." The independence of these Appalachian people who wanted to be left alone to work their land was put to the test when the government decided that the liquor should be taxed. This same sentiment had gripped the people in 1794, during the Whiskey Rebellion, when people revolted against the government, which was attempting to tax home-distilled spirits.

In May 1876, the North Carolina area of Dark Corner was introduced to the national psyche when Lewis Redmond shot U.S. deputy marshal Alfred

Modern-day view of the Dark Corner. *Photograph by John Stoy.*

Duckworth, who was trying to serve Redmond with a warrant. Redmond had a good business for himself, making whiskey and distributing for others. Redmond soon fled to Pickens County. Newspapers across the South hailed him a folk hero who had acted "for a noble cause." The dark-haired, rugged mountain man was an instant celebrity. A dime novel called *Entwined Lives* featured "Redmond the Outlaw," and he was portrayed as a "Wild Bill" type, complete with flowing blond locks, a handsome face and bookshelves that attested to his "culture and refinement." In the northern papers, he was depicted as an uncouth, slovenly marauder—a land pirate of few morals. In April 1881, Redmond was shot several times by revenuers and was thought to be dead, but the hardy man survived, adding to his legend. That August, he pled guilty in Greenville to eight charges of being in violation of the internal revenue laws and two charges of conspiracy. With public sympathy, along with the favor of Governor Wade Hampton, Lewis Redmond received a presidential pardon from Chester Arthur on May 16, 1884, resulting in a kind of mountain justice being played out repeatedly in the Dark Corner. In 1886, the government hired him to run a legal distillery in Walhalla, a job he did well until he retired in 1905. Lewis Redmond died in 1906 at the age of fifty-one in Walhalla.

Harper's Weekly depiction of "Moonshiners, 8 Men With Rifles in Woods, 1878." *Courtesy of the Library of Congress.*

THE STILL LIFE

Moonshining was a family affair, a skill and trade handed down through several generations like a royal title. Rivalries were frequent, and those who wanted to corner the market for themselves often ratted out other distillers to the law. Many of the "revenooers" and lawmen were locals, putting them at odds with former neighbors and friends. One such light in the Dark Corner was Sheriff Perry Duncan Gilreath. Gilreath was elected sheriff in 1876, the same year Wade Hampton (the great-grandson of Anthony Hampton of the Hampton Massacre) became governor of South Carolina. Gilreath was well respected, even by the outlaws, and he rarely carried a gun. In a time when a man's word was his bond, Gilreath relied on common sense and treated people with dignity—such was the case with a mountaineer outlaw called Hub Garmany. Old Hub had found himself in a pickle in February 1877, after a gunfight with Deputy Marshal Van Buren Hendrix resulted in the death of the lawman.

Armed with just a warrant, Gilreath set out into the hills to bring Garmany to jail. After a reasonable conversation with Garmany's father, Gilreath learned that he was hiding along a stream among dense thickets. As Gilreath made his way through the thick brush, Garmany called out a warning to not come any closer. Garmany was behind a large oak tree with a gun and was desperate to not be caught. Gilreath sat and told Garmany that he just wanted to talk. Garmany listened to the benevolent man, and after a while, he dropped his gun, telling Gilreath that he would trust him. Gilreath took Garmany to his own home, fed him a home-cooked supper and provided him with lodging for the night before taking him to jail the next morning. Hub Garmany was acquitted by the jury, which found that he had acted in self-defense.

Also in February 1877, former Dark Corner distiller turned revenue agent Tom Johnson shot and killed the child of Jackson Ward as he was being carried in his father's arms during a raid. Johnson, then considered a turncoat by his neighbors, claimed he didn't see the boy, and he was acquitted by a jury of his peers, including Hub Garmany.

A party of about eight revenue officers conducted a raid on April 19, 1878, with the intention of wrecking a known still. After destroying some mash, the party split up, suspecting that the still had already been moved. Marshal Rufus Springs was alone when shots rang out and hit him. Since that party had separated, Springs was alone when he fell on his face, leaving no witnesses. The men laid Springs across his horse and brought him back to town. Dr. Waddy Thompson (the grandson of Waddy Thompson of nullification-era fame) testified that the bullet wound would have been sufficient to kill Springs in half a minute. Springs's killer was never found.

A kindness can be fatal, like in the sad case of Deputy Marshal John D. Kirby. Kirby and his officers seized about sixty gallons of whiskey, along with its makers, Joseph Dill and his son, "Little John," in 1896. On the journey to Spartanburg Jail, Kirby felt bad for the elder Dill and unlocked his handcuffs. Little John, who had put up quite a fight during his arrest, pleaded with Kirby to unlock his cuffs also and promised he would be good.

The officers stopped for breakfast at Holly Springs Baptist Church, after which, three of the deputies rode on

Sheriff Perry Duncan Gilreath in his retirement years. *Courtesy of the Greenville County Library.*

ahead, leaving Kirby and one other officer to tend to the Dills. The Dills returned to the wagon after their meal, with Little John then uncuffed. Kirby directed them to get back in the wagon while his Winchester was set against the wagon, unattended. Little John grabbed the rifle and turned it on Kirby, stating that he wasn't going any farther. Kirby stepped forward and was shot through the head; he dropped instantly. Threatening the same for the other officers, father and son escaped on foot.

The next day, the Dills arrived in Greenville at the law office of J. Allender Moody. Little John told Moody he had acted in self-defense and that his father had nothing to do with it. He wanted to take his chances on being tried in Greenville instead of Spartanburg County, where the crime had taken place. Little John lost his bid for the venue and was tried in Spartanburg, but Moody was a good lawyer, and the jury had doubts. Little John was found guilty of manslaughter, served a short sentence and returned to the Dark Corner. He died in 1938 as a bachelor at the age of sixty-four in the home of his sister Nancy Forest in Greensboro, North Carolina.

As the moonshine industry flourished during Prohibition, mountaineers in the Dark Corner were making good money, sending liquor across state lines and into big cities, like Chicago. Families were torn between the illicit trade and the crime it brought to the community and their own interests. One such torn man was James Holland Howard. Holland Howard had come from a family steeped in generational whiskey making: he was the great-grandson of Captain Thomas Howard, who had been led through the mountains by Skyuka some years earlier.

Howard was trying to be a legitimate farmer, living his life in a good, Christian manner. He was a regular volunteer state constable and had recently destroyed the still of his nephew H.S. Howard in a raid on Glassy Mountain. On January 31, 1924, Howard was assisting Federal Agent Reuben Gosnell, another local whose family had lived in the remote mountains for years and knew everyone and their business. Earlier that morning, they had caught the moonshining Plumley brothers and were holding them in a corncrib guarded by Clarence Howard (Holland Howard's son) and an agent named Austin. Leaving the younger Howard and Austin to guard the Plumleys, Holland and Gosnell went to seek out a still that they were sure belonged to Alex Pittman. "Alec" was well known to both men as a neighbor and regular flouter of Prohibition laws. At about 12:00 p.m., while on the way to the still, Holland identified two hats in a nearby camp as belonging to Alec and his son Fred Pittman. Gosnell hid himself in a thicket while Howard took the other side. Howard sprang into action, taking the whiskey makers by surprise, and he called out, "Reuben, come," to his partner when shots rang out. Two men ran in opposite directions, and Gosnell gave chase to the man closest to him. The man who was being chased was running out of breath when he turned around to shoot his pursuer. Gosnell tackled a man to the ground, who turned out to be twenty-one-year-old Holland Pittman, another son of Alec's, with an unfired .45. Holland Howard had been gunned down, shot five times, front and back, with his gun lying on the ground, the hammer on an empty chamber. Gosnell remanded Holland Pittman and walked with him back to the corncrib to inform Clarence Howard that his father was dead. He then arranged for the young Howard to take the Plumleys to Greenville. Gosnell and Holland Pittman walked back to the still, where they were fired at. Gosnell told Pittman to tell him who the shooter was before they were all killed, or Gosnell would shoot him himself. Pittman offered up the name Henry Lindsay. On the way to the jail in Greenville, Holland Pittman made a passing remark to an officer named Smith that he guessed he would be going to the electric chair. Alec Pittman was arrested a few days later.

The trial of Alec and Holland Pittman brought much excitement to the area. The *Greenville News* could hardly contain its merriment, proclaiming headlines like "Latest Tragedy Promises to Be Thrilling Case" and "Famous Dark Corner of County Has Produced Another Sensational Murder Case in Killing of J.H. Howard." Like a court in some banana republic, the evidence was laid out thusly:

- Holland Howard had recognized the hat of Alex Pittman at a camp a quarter of a mile from the still (the crime scene).
- Footprints, identified by Wade Plumley, two days later at the still were said to be those of Alex Pittman.
- Holland Pittman made a remark to an officer about getting the electric chair.

And that was it. It did not matter that the gun Holland Pittman had had not been fired; the other man seen running in the opposite direction of the crime scene could not be named by Gosnell, and Henry Lindsay was never investigated. Alec Pittman testified that he was at home, shucking corn, an alibi sworn to in an affidavit by H.S. Howard, Holland Howard's nephew, who testified that he had been by Pittman's home around 11:30 a.m. and that he was there. While Alec's wife and Holland's mother, Martha, wept in court, the jury found the father and son guilty and sentenced them to die in the electric chair. Years of looking the other way when it came to the deeds of these mountaineers had come to an end. Already sentenced to death by the press, Alec and Holland Pittman would pay for their crimes of being moonshiners.

Stills were a "breeding place for crime," as spelled out in a letter to the editor of the *Greenville News* on February 17, 1924, written by the grieving son of Holland Howard, Jim, a ministerial student and football star at Furman University. The sentiment of the hurting child and much of the community was spelled out on page 1. He said the moonshiner was not the only one to blame—his customers carried some of the burden as well:

> *The man that buys a keg of whiskey and transports it to town transports more than whiskey alone. He transports that which causes sorrow, heartaches, tears, empty pocketbooks, poverty-stricken homes, ignorance, preventable diseases and immorality.*

The Pittmans maintained their innocence, and the newspapers continued to write about them. An extensive puff piece in Orangeburg's *Times and Democrat's* November 7, 1925 edition announced the jailhouse nuptials

Mr. and Mrs. Holland Pittman, 1926. *Author's collection.*

of Rosemary Keenan (nineteen) and her childhood sweetheart, Holland Pittman. The paper reported that Rosemary had been at college at the time of the crime, and she believed that he did not do it. Her faith helped her remain strong, and her family could not keep her away from her death row love. The article told the Romeo and Juliet–like tale of Keenan's forbidden romance, her family banning her from any contact with the mountain boy.

"So, knowing that he must die, knowing that their married life would be but a series of visits, twice each week to the county jail, where she could see him for a minute through the bars and give him her message of love in the presence of witnesses, Rosemary Keenan became Mrs. Holland Pittman."

In January 1925, the Pittmans' lawyers had filed a motion for a new trial, saying that the evidence presented at the original trial had been circumstantial at best. The motion was denied. The newlywed Mrs. Holland Pittman went on to declare in January 1926 that she was the shooter of Constable Howard—making great copy but going nowhere in the courts.

On October 15, 1926, the Pittmans were due to be executed, but South Carolina governor Thomas McLeod granted a stay while he reviewed the case and converted their terms to life in prison, blaming their condition on society and lamenting that mountain folk were not properly taught right from wrong. Life imprisonment being ostensibly less attractive than condemnation, Rosemary Pittman was soon in the wind, likely reinventing herself in parts unknown, and she was never heard from again.

Society apparently failed once again, when, in April 1927, Martha Pittman and her and Alec's other sons, Eli and Fred, were charged with violating Prohibition law. Martha received a slap on the wrist, and the boys were sent to reform school.

Father and son continued as model prisoners; newspapers frequently ran stories about their work in prison, making quilt covers, working in the machine shop, all the while fighting for clemency that was repeatedly denied. In February 1929, Alec had an operation in which his left foot had to be amputated. The aging man was granted a weeklong furlough in April 1930, and he returned to Dark Corner and much fanfare from family and friends.

Also in 1930, Clarence Howard, the son of Holland Howard who guarded the Plumleys in the corncrib that fateful day, was gunned down himself in a raid in North Carolina, where he worked as a dry agent and driver for the feds—meeting the same fate as his father.

Fred Pittman continued to appeal to the governor throughout the early 1930s before finally securing parole for his father and brother in October 1933. The *Gaffney Ledger* proclaimed, "Eight Years' Service, Father and Son Free."

Holland remarried in 1934 and started a family, living until 1981. Alec died in 1939. They were both buried in the Mount Pleasant Baptist Church Cemetery in the Glassy Mountain area of Dark Corner.

A TALE OF TWO BILLS

A biting cold air whipped through the mountains on a February evening in 1888. Benjamin Ross warmed himself by his hearth; earlier in the day, he had a meeting with Commissioner Hawthorne, in which he had stated he was ready to publicly tell what he knew about an upcoming whiskey hearing. It was rumored that Ross had led revenue officers to a secret still that they never would have located themselves. The barrel of a gun through a hole in Ross's wall that evening made sure that he would never talk again.

Sheriff P.D. Gilreath went through a list in his mind of who would benefit from the silencing of Ben Ross, and he immediately suspected the Howard clan. The Howards had been a fixture in Dark Corner since the Cherokee wars. Armed with warrants for "Little Bill" and "Big Bill" Howard, Gilreath made his way into the mountains. The Howards faced Gilreath, armed with their pistols, and they told the sheriff that they couldn't make it to jail that day. Gilreath asked them when they could make it, and they promised to turn themselves in on Monday morning at 8:00 a.m. sharp. As promised, come Monday morning, they arrived at the Greenville Jail and booked into custody.

Little Bill, who happened to be Benjamin Ross's nephew (most of these people are related in one way or another, by the way), confessed to the shooting but pinned the architecture of the crime on his cousin Big Bill. In July 1890, a jury acquitted Big Bill and sentenced Little Bill to be hanged on September 26, 1890. Little Bill was twenty-two years old, a newlywed and a new father. His wife/cousin, Mary, would travel to Greenville Jail every Saturday with the baby in tow to visit her husband. It was said that she would wear homemade dresses and a big sun bonnet and would make the twenty-seven-mile trek by foot or hitch a ride if she was lucky enough to see a passing wagon. Jailers would let her stay with Little Bill until Monday morning, when she would make the journey back to the mountains. This went on for months, as Little Bill had been granted a stay on appeal. Every Saturday, the jailer would let Mary and baby in, and every Monday morning, he would get up and let her out before going back to bed. During one such routine, the jailer let Mary and the baby out and noticed that she was walking in a funny way, but he shrugged it off and went back to bed, figuring it was the many miles she had walked. A few hours later, the jailer brought Little Bill his breakfast to discover Mary in bed wrapped in the jail blanket! Little Bill had busted out with the baby, dressed in the sun bonnet and dress like a character in a Buster Keaton movie.

Publisher A.B. Williams, a good friend of Sheriff Gilreath, told the *Greenville News*, as recounted in the book *P.D. Gilreath High Sheriff*:

> *Little Bill had stopped at a friend's house, left the baby and his wife's dress and sun bonnet and dug out for tall timber. Catch him? Give a mountaineer and a Howard two hours clear start in that county and catch him? You might as well try to catch a flash of lightning in a tin dipper.*

Mary Howard was sent home. Williams explained that they "they couldn't have raked up a jury to convict."

With Little Bill on the lam, George Center was brooding over the murder of his stepfather, Ben Ross. His ire was directed at Big Bill Howard, not his little sidekick. Center and Big Bill were first cousins and grew up, at times, in the same household together.

According to author Dean Campbell, Center confronted Big Bill on a mountain road in December 1890. Center accused Big Bill of trying to "hire Little Bill to kill me." Big Bill denied the accusation but said he liked the idea. Big Bill went for his pocket while dismounting his mule. Center feared for his life and shot Big Bill with a Remington rifle.

Fellow mountaineer Bill Moon heard the shot and arrived to find Big Bill lying in the road, gasping for air. Center told Moon he had shot him in self-defense. Moon sent for the renowned area doctor, Dr. William Mooney, who found a knife in Big Bill's hand. Big Bill was taken to his home to be made comfortable; he named George Center as his shooter before dying from his gunshot wound the next day.

Center had it relayed to Gilreath that he would surrender at Glassy Mountain Church on an agreed day and time. When the sheriff arrived to arrest Center, he found only Big Bill's brothers ready to kill the no-show. Gilreath eventually caught Center, who was remanded with a promise of safety.

Little Bill spent a great deal of time back in the Dark Corner after his daring escape, and Gilreath knew where he was. Perhaps Gilreath didn't agree with his death sentence, or maybe he was amused at his great escape. All might have been forgotten and forgiven, but Little Bill couldn't stop running his mouth and was often seen at stills, sometimes in the light of day, bragging that no sheriff could catch the likes of him. Gilreath was no fool and was not going to be made a fool of, so he saddled up his horse and traveled into the mountains to arrest Little Bill.

After midnight on February 24, 1891, Gilreath and Deputy James Moon, along with two other men, reached the house of Little Bill's father-in-law, William Ross. Gilreath planned to have two of the men go behind the house and wait for a signal to make enough noise to give them the impression that a group larger than two was waiting at the rear of the cabin. Ross opened the door to reveal Gilreath and Moon. Gilreath said that he had come with a posse of men to arrest Bill Howard. Gilreath shouted, "He's here, men. Look out for him and shoot him if he comes out!" Gilreath and Moon entered the cabin and asked Ross where Little Bill was. Ross pointed to a shed room but said that Little Bill was well armed and in the room with two other men, his brother Mitch and Bill Moon, who was probably related to the deputy. Little Bill yelled through the door that he would shoot whoever opened the door. He was prepared to not be taken alive. Gilreath told Little Bill that he would certainly kill him as his duty required but that he did not want to. In his fatherly manner, Gilreath talked through the door, urging Bill to surrender and face jail—maybe he would be cleared, or maybe he would hang, but he should face it as a man of honor. Twenty minutes or so went by, and Little Bill said he would surrender to Gilreath—and only Gilreath. So, Gilreath opened the door and placed him under arrest. Little Bill soon realized that the posse consisted of only four men and became enraged, but it was too late. Mary had been in the house the entire time and wailed, her heart broken at the prospect of losing her husband again. Gilreath let Little Bill say goodbye to her and then took him directly to Greenville Jail.

Little Bill was held in the same jail as George Center. He was granted a new trial and was acquitted. George Center was found innocent by reason of self-defense. The lands were again theirs.

HOLY REVENGE

In September 1891, Mountain Hill Church was described by the *Manning Times* of Manning, South Carolina, as "a rude place of worship used by foot-washing Baptists in the heart of the Blue Ridge Mountains." *Rude* was an apt descriptor for this crudely constructed log cabin; slats in the wood allowed natural light to stream in, along with any other flying or creeping thing that might penetrate the exposed areas of the walls. Nevertheless, it was as good a place to worship as any for Dark Corner residents. Its appearance resembled many of their homes, and they liked it just fine. In *To Kill a Mockingbird*, Harper Lee's character Miss Maudie tells Scout that Boo Radley's father is a "foot-washing Baptist" and that "footwashers believe anything that's a pleasure is a sin." This puritanical view of the Appalachian Mountain dwellers seems an unlikely description for this congregation, considering events that took place at the church on the stifling Sunday of August 23, 1891.

Joshua Howard felt the world was against him. This personal grievance gnawed at his heart, and he was an angry young man. His brother Massena had done well for himself and married a refined-looking woman who bore him a son. Massena had tried to set a decent example for his troubled brother and was relieved when Joshua was hired as a farmhand by the Durhams, but Arry Durham worried about the influence Joshua had on his youngest son, Rufus, the one the family called "Babe," and he soon let the young Joshua go.

Babe Durham was a drunk and a psychotic; a perceived sideways glance from you, and he wanted you dead. In January 1891, Babe had gone on a crime spree, whipping a "little deaf and dumb negro boy" within an inch of his life, shooting another Black man named Jesse Sample, whipping another child and then shooting at a crowded wagon; but lady justice didn't seem in a hurry to look at this wayward Durham boy, and poor Hildia Gosnell would soon pay the price.

Babe had fancied himself in love with the plain but pretty mountain girl. Her father, Richard Gosnell, was the patriarch of a large Glassy Mountain family and a deacon of the church. Babe had set his heart on marrying the young Miss Gosnell, but she did not reciprocate his feelings and pledged her love to John Bridgeman, the younger brother of Sherman, who married her older sister. This was too much for Babe to think about, so during a church service in July 1891, he beat her to a bloody pulp with the butt of his gun, and she almost died. The small community had come to know this as "Babe's way," and like a spoiled child, he received no punishment.

All this bad blood culminated on that Sunday, August 23, 1891. Joshua Howard waited outside the church that morning, when Richard Gosnell entered. When Gosnell did not greet Joshua, he took this as a personal affront. Luther Durham tried to diffuse the situation, but Joshua pulled a .22 out and shot Luther's tongue in two before shooting him in the bowels. Armed Howards, Durhams, Bridgemans and Gosnells flooded into the churchyard.

When all was said and done, it was estimated that between forty and fifty rounds flew in all directions. In the end, Joshua and Messena Howard were dead, and two Howards were wounded, but Luther Durham managed to survive, as did Sherman Bridgeman, after receiving a round to the head.

The inquest was a fiasco; accounts varied about who shot whom. Sherman Bridgeman, Richard Gosnell and Babe Durham were put on trial. Massena's wife testified that Massena didn't want anything to do with it and that he had told her, "If they kill one another, let them do it." She did not see who shot her husband but claimed that with his dying breath, Massena had named Babe Durham. The jury concluded that Sherman Bridgeman had shot Joshua, after which they concluded no one was guilty.

In 1959, ninety-year-old resident Mattie Pierce recalled that the congregation was singing "There's a Great Day Coming" when Josh and Massie Howard were killed: "There's a great day coming, a great day coming, there's a great day coming by and by, when the saints and the sinners shall be parted right and left. Are you ready for that day to come?"

DEATH TAKES THE STAND

An argument and a gallon of whiskey are two ingredients that, when combined, can create a recipe for disaster. That is what was cooking in May 1919, when Alex Campbell shot his employee James Garvin dead with a shotgun.

Testimony told the story of Garvin, an employee on Campbell's farm in Gowensville. He was a surly drunk who, when confronted by Campbell's eight-year-old son, threatened him with a gun. Campbell testified that he and Garvin were finishing up work when it began to rain, and they took up refuge in the storehouse. His son had also come into the storehouse and was playing when he picked up a pair of overalls and presented them to Garvin, saying, "Here's a pair of pants for you." This set Garvin off, and he held a gun up to the little boy's ribs. Campbell got his shotgun from under the eaves and shot Garvin in the head. He died instantly. Campbell obtained a lawyer and turned himself in the next day. It was found that Campbell had acted in self-defense, and he was released.

Campbell continued to toil away on his farm, where he lived with his wife, Tallie Center Campbell, and their eight children. On the evening of March 25, 1932, Campbell shot his wife in the back, apparently in a drunken stupor. He claimed he had no recollection of the event. Surgery was performed on

The grave of Tallie Center Campbell next to the grave of her husband at Ebenezer Welcome Baptist Church Cemetery. *Photograph by John Stoy.*

Tallie at Black Hospital in Spartanburg, where she hung on in considerable pain until she died on April 1. She was thirty-nine years old.

At the inquest, a picture was painted of an argument between the husband and wife, and it was testified to by witness C.W. Painter. Painter explained that he and Campbell had been drinking together throughout the day and that they had arrived at the Campbell residence about 10:00 p.m. Mrs. Campbell told her husband that Prohibition agents had been to the house earlier that day, looking for their son, and she told Campbell it was all his fault. An angry Campbell called her a liar, got his pistol and fired the fateful shot. Their daughter Erline Campbell backed up Painter's story, and Campbell received a life sentence for the murder of his wife.

In 1935, Campbell was granted parole, and in 1937, he found himself back in court, facing charges of illicit distilling. While on the stand in U.S. District Court, he was asked if he knew another defendant in the case. Campbell answered that he "would know him in hell." He seemed to take his statement quite literally, as he immediately stiffened and slumped into his seat, dying then and there of heart failure.

THE BURIED SECRET

"In a dream, the strangest and the oddest things appear. And what insane and silly things we do. Here is what I see before me, vividly and clear, as I recall it. You were in it, too." Those are the opening lyrics to "I Had the Craziest Dream," the number-one song in early 1943 by Harry James and his Orchestra with Helen Forrest. But it wasn't a dream when Paul Thompson arrived at the sheriff's office to report that his mother was missing. Paul was concerned that no one had seen her in four days. His father, Lee, who was prone to regular bouts of drunkenness, had no idea where she could be. Sheriff Homer Bearden had a strange feeling and assigned a few deputies and the coroner to go out to the homestead in Gowensville, not far from Campbell's Covered Bridge.

Mollie Elizabeth Thompson (née Turner) had been born in Campobello in 1886 and had been married to her husband, Alvin Lee Thompson, for thirty-seven years. They had raised three children together. The couple lived in Spartanburg for a time before moving back to the area that was in the shadow of Dark Corner. Alcohol was easy to come by in those parts, and Lee partook regularly. Mollie was opposed to drinking, and this caused constant arguments between them. He had tried to quit on several occasions, even once going sober for a year before falling off the wagon again. Not long before Mollie disappeared, Thompson had been robbed during a drinking spree. He was so embarrassed that he had put himself in that situation that he tried to take his own life with a rifle, and he carried a scar on the left shoulder of his large frame.

On April 11, sixteen days after Mollie Thompson had gone missing, the Thompsons' home burned down between 4:00 and 6:00 a.m. Neighbors reported that household items had been moved out by relatives, leaving the house virtually bare. Bearden led a search party of deputies and volunteers, including Lee Thompson, in combing the wooded countryside. Nearby resident Jess Allen came across a plot of freshly disturbed dirt under some brush near his home. Moving the dirt with a stick, he discovered a shoe sticking out. A little more prodding, and he saw that a foot was still in it. Mollie had been hastily buried in a four-by-three-foot grave while fully clothed and wrapped in a sheet. She had been shot with a .32-caliber rifle at close range; the bullet entered the back of her head and exited over her right eye. Mr. Thompson, who had been assisting in the search, suddenly went missing himself.

News traveled fast among the locals, and a manhunt turned up Thompson a day later. He had been hiding under some hay in a barn but was in bad shape. He had tried to slash his own throat and was taken to the hospital. Officers combed through the charred ruins of the Thompsons' home, looking for clues, while waiting for Thompson to recover for questioning. He was being kept under heavy guard. When the bewhiskered man could finally speak, he confessed from his hospital bed that he had been drunk for several days when he had asked Mollie to fix him some breakfast. When she refused, he became angry and grabbed his rifle. He shot a few times to "scare her" but hit her on the third shot. He panicked and didn't know what to do, so he hid her in a closet where she remained for a "day and night." In his drunken state, he thought he would get away with his crime. He took $115 from inside her shirt, pinned near her bosom, and buried her. While the search party was looking for her, he thought the brush had been moved from the mountainside grave and ran into the woods behind Ernest Good's house. He had a razor in his overcoat, which he used to cut his throat. It started to rain, and he crawled to Good's barn, unable to walk. He was found a few hours later by Good and others. He didn't know anything about the house fire until he got to the barn, and he said he had nothing to do with it. Then sober, Thompson didn't feel he deserved any mercy, telling deputies, "No one had anything to do with the killing and burying of my wife but myself, and no one knew anything about it whatsoever except me." A few days later, still under the watchful eye of a guard at the general hospital, Thompson confessed, after "the Lord got ahold of me," that he had paid an accomplice to assist with his wife's burial. Tobe Allen, a fifty-year-old Black man, was charged. Thompson alleged that Allen had helped him dig the grave and then carry Mollie from the closet to the hole for $25.

After being examined and cleared at the state mental hospital, Thompson was found competent to stand trial in September. While his three adult children watched from the front row, Thompson recounted the horrible events surrounding the death of his wife. While nervously twirling his hat in his hands, Thompson maintained that the shooting had been an accident. Tears streamed down his face and rolled off his nose. "The killing all seemed like a dream to me—a dull dream." Thompson was asked if Mollie had been a good wife; he answered that she had been, adding, "I loved her." Thompson explained to the court that he had tried to stop drinking on several occasions and that when he was in that state, Mollie refused to cook for him. He didn't know right from wrong in his hazy mindset and did not intentionally aim the gun at her. As Mollie's body lay in the closet for more than a day, Thompson continued his drinking binge, downing both legal and illegal whiskey.

The day Mollie was found, he hid in some woods that belonged to Ernest Good—but not before returning to the house to get an overcoat and razor. "I wanted to end it all. I didn't want anybody to see me."

A previous arrest of Thompson for drunkenness and treatment for a "mental disorder" some fifteen years prior also came to light at the trial. Thompson's children, Irvin, Paul and Lucille Thompson Pittman, testified that their parents had a good relationship, except when their father "took to drink."

The jury deliberated for a little less than two hours before reaching a guilty verdict but asked the court for mercy. The judge sentenced the six-foot-tall, two-hundred-pound man, described as a "mountaineer" in the press, to life in prison.

Tobe Allen went to trial in December and was charged as an accessory, which he denied any knowledge of from the stand. Allen convinced the jury, and he was acquitted.

Paul, who had reported his mother missing all those years ago, dropping the first domino in a living nightmare, was listed as the informant on Lee Thompson's death certificate after he died of cerebral thrombosis due to cardiovascular disease while serving on a Greenville County chain gang on June 2, 1963.

4

THE NEW SOUTH

*G*reenville saw a population boom in the early twentieth century. A metropolis for manufacturing, the mills employed many of the town's residents, and increases in suburban development accommodated white and Black citizens alike. Middle-class working women were regular sights in shops, stores and offices. A convergence of Jewish and Greek immigrants also arrived in town at the turn of the century, incorporating into society and building churches and synagogues.

The *Greenville News* ran a piece on January 10, 1910, about the "Obliterating of the Red-Light District" to make way for railroad tracks near Fall Street and McBee Avenue. The paper hoped that the few citizens who were holding out on selling their properties would soon change their minds and that the "denizens of these dives of degradation would seek quarters out of the city limits." The article cheered on the forthcoming "pretty structure" that was to be erected by the railroad company to replace "the inmates of the underworld."

Trolley lines soon expanded into the suburbs, and the first automobiles began to appear. Movie theaters and department stores soon sprung up as Greenville approached the Jazz Age.

The textile mill communities entertained the city with a baseball league, which produced a star in Joseph Jackson. "Shoeless Joe" grew up at Brandon Mill and played on the team there until he was recruited for the Greenville Spinners. He eventually played in the MLB, where he was embroiled in the

Black Sox Scandal (Shoeless Joe and others were accused of "throwing the 1919 World Series" in exchange for money). Joe was eventually acquitted but was banned for life from the Baseball Hall of Fame. Joe's legacy is still alive and well in Greenville; his former home was moved downtown, near Flour Field, home of the MiLB team the Greenville Drive, and became the Shoeless Joe Jackson Museum. His grave at Woodlawn Memorial Park is still frequented by visitors, who leave shoes and baseballs.

THE PRETTY GREER'S WOMAN

"Mama, don't shoot Papa," seven-year-old Leo Hughes begged his mother, but Mattie was leveling a revolver at her husband, George Washington Hughes. She glanced at the clock; she'd given him two minutes to fight or die like a dog.

George Hughes had been a successful blacksmith in Reidville when he met the fifteen-year-old brunette beauty Mattie Waldrop. Her father, Isaac Waldrop, was on the lam for running a speakeasy and was probably headed to Mexico when Mattie agreed to marry the besotted thirty-year-old Hughes. Friends of Hughes tried to warn him against the match, as they could tell she was trouble and would try to "wear the breeches" in the relationship, but Hughes had stars in his eyes. The small town of Reidville was not glamorous enough for Mattie, and the couple moved to Greer around 1888. There, Hughes became a successful merchant. She had a scrape with the law during a "local scandal," but details are scant.

Time was up. Mattie fired a shot, and Hughes went down to the floor. The family cook rushed in to find that Mattie had shot Hughes in front of their young son. The cook later testified that the couple fought regularly, and that Mattie was violent. The final fracture that evening had been an accusation of Mattie's infidelity by Hughes.

Several days before the murder, Mattie had deposited a large sum of money into her personal bank account and had sold off stocks in a local factory and mill. Hughes and Leo had been sleeping in the upstairs bedroom, and Mattie had been sleeping downstairs. The night of the shooting, Mattie had secured a one-hundred-dollar bill in her pocket and had tied up their horse and buggy at the front gate.

Hughes lived through the night and stated that his wife had shot him on purpose, adding that he would never hurt her and that "there is not a woman on earth that I cared for but her." The cook overheard Mattie tell Hughes that the shooting was accidental, and he told her that she knew it was not. Hughes died the next morning, on November 19, 1898. After the arrival of Sheriff Jeff Davis Gilreath and Coroner Wilbanks, Mattie rifled through her husband's pockets and emptied them before she was taken to the Greenville Jail.

Wilbanks held an inquest on November 23, and it was determined, "[Mattie], willfully and feloniously, did kill the said George W. Hughes, against the peace and dignity of the state aforesaid."

The trial created quite a stir in March 1899, and crowds gathered to get a look at the pretty "self-made widow." Columbia's *State* newspaper, on March 24, described Mattie dressed in her "widow's weeds":

> *Her attire today was most tasteful. A widow's black bonnet and veil were fastened to her wavy, brown hair with mourning hairpins. Her gown was a close-fitting black garment that displayed to perfection her neat, trim figure, while everything else about her attire was in the best of taste, black kid gloves, watch chain and handkerchief all matching. The dark costume heightened the effect of the ruddy complexion, and her brown eyes sparkled beneath long, languorous lashes. There are elements of beauty in her face, but it is her appearance that strikes one. Her expression is not without a naughty twinkle of the eye, and as she stood in the dock, she nonchalantly chewed a wee bit of gum, coolly taking in all the proceedings.*

After the laborious task of gathering a jury, the trial lasted a week. Witnesses testified to recurrent quarrelling in the home, with regular threats of violence from Mattie. Upon the arrival of the cook directly after the shooting, Mattie had announced, "Damn him. He's not hurt much." It was revealed that as Hughes lay dying in bed, Mattie had kissed him, to which he said, "Mattie, that is the first time you have kissed me in two years." Mattie took the stand in her own defense, recounting her accidental shooting tale. After several hours of deliberation, the case was declared a mistrial. Mattie quipped to the press, "Well, a mistrial is better than a conviction!"

The second trial began in June, and Mattie was put on the stand for nearly three hours. She maintained a languid delivery of her innocence, punctuated with emotional tears. The state persisted that she had not even been affected that night, which she denied, saying, "If I was not troubled and distressed that night, I don't know what trouble is." Trial number two also ended in a mistrial.

118 North Main Street, where Mattie Hughes lived and ran a brothel. *Photograph by John Stoy.*

By the time the third trial had begun in September 1899, public interest had also begun to wane. Mattie was yesterday's news; those who sat in the half-filled courtroom seats were party to a dying statement from Hughes, which had been taken down by Reverend D.B. Sampson and not been allowed in the earlier trials. The deathbed deposition recounted that Mattie had threatened to kill Hughes while little Leo pleaded for his life. Hughes stated that he made this statement knowing he was going to die, and that Mattie had pulled a pistol on him "at least a dozen times." The papers thought the statement was a doozy and that it would cement the fate of justice finding the black widow. But alas, a third mistrial caused the state to finally take a nolle prosequi (forget it, we give up), and Mattie was free.[*]

The grave of George Washington Hughes at Edgewood Cemetery in Greer. *Photograph by John Stoy.*

In 1900, Leo was being raised in Spartanburg by a Hughes uncle while Mattie ran a restaurant and lived with her father at 118 North Main Street before getting in trouble for running a brothel there in 1901. Mattie skipped her court appearance and was seen about town in men's clothing before eventually landing in Washington, D.C., under the assumed name "Frankie Harris." In 1911, Frankie was arrested for running three bordellos and eventually disappeared until reports of her death surfaced in 1915.

Mattie had evidently come home and surprised some robbers who beat her, stole her jewelry and shot her, along with her father and a companion named Nicholas Coffinas. While Mattie's father, Isaac Waldrop, and lover, Coffinas, were indeed dead, the papers got it wrong about Mattie. Mattie survived her injuries and lived another twenty-five years. Mattie Hughes died as a patient in the psychiatric hospital St. Elizabeth's in Washington, D.C., on December 6, 1941. She is buried at Oakwood Cemetery in Falls Church, Virginia.

---

[*] *Nolle prosequi* is a Latin phrase meaning "will no longer prosecute," per www.nolo.com, a legal encyclopedia.

George Washington Hughes was buried in Greer under an ornate monument in the Edgewood Cemetery. George and Mattie's son, Leo Charles Hughes, went on to lead a productive life as the manager of a coal company in West Virginia, where he fathered ten children of his own and died in 1975 at the age of eighty-three.

OVER THE EDGE

George Heldmann often bragged that his father had been a Prussian soldier in the battle at Waterloo. The German native had come to Greenville in 1846, married a local girl named Matilda and became a successful saddle and harness maker at the corner of Broad and South Main Streets. His Greenville home and business had a perfect view of the courthouse, and despite his wealth, Heldmann would charge admission for spectators to view the latest public hanging.

At the end of 1888, Heldmann and his wife were having a tough time with their only child, Fannie. Fannie was twenty-five years old and engaged to be married. What should have been a happy time in their lives was a source of worry. A darkness had enveloped Fannie, fragmenting her mind, and her parents feared she had become insane. They resorted to locking her away in a bedroom. The future groom was never named in the press or any official documents. Research reveals one of the candidates was a young lawyer, while others mention that he was a business associate of her father's. Whoever the young suitor was, he did not appeal to Fannie. For reasons only known to her, she did not want to marry this man.

On the eve of the new year in 1889, Fannie slipped out of her imprisonment and ran to the Reedy River. After discovering she had escaped, Heldmann took off in pursuit. He broke several ribs in the process when he fell on a railroad trestle. Fannie's lifeless body was later found in the Reedy River, where she had managed to drown herself in water that came up to her knees.

The sorrowful Heldmanns had a monument befitting a princess erected at Springwood Cemetery. Heldmann would join his daughter there in 1892, later followed by Matilda in 1900. Matilda left an estate worth $650,000 to her remaining siblings.

While money couldn't buy Fannie's happiness, could it have saved the little beggar boy?

Left: Fannie Heldmann, circa 1888. *Courtesy of Susan Truett Hovermale.*

Right: The memorial for Fannie Heldmann at Springwood Cemetery. *Photograph by John Stoy.*

Weaver Smith was nine years old and a familiar sight in the neighborhood around Springwood Cemetery. A notorious panhandler, Smith was known to most of the area's households, as they often gave food scraps to him. In the first week of November 1898, downtown Greenville received an influx of troops to shore up U.S. defenses in the Spanish-American War. Despite a vicious cold snap, soldiers were soon bustling all over town, delighting the local merchants. The *Mountaineer* proclaimed that the soldiers gave Greenville "a livelier look." Not so lively, however, was the body of a little boy that was discovered in some shrubs on Elrod Street, across from the cemetery, in the early morning of November 18. A Black woman recognized the boy as Weaver Smith. Smith was covered in gore. The little boy, who was once loved by a mother, had been sodomized, strangled and stabbed, his stomach ripped open and his entrails strewn across the ground. Newspapers quickly dubbed Smith the "Little Beggar Boy."

Mr. Riser, the sexton of the Springwood Cemetery, had fed Smith supper early in the evening, and then he was seen hanging around the soldiers at the north side camp. Two New York soldiers claimed they had seen the boy in the company of an unknown soldier later that night.

The governor put up a reward for any information leading to an arrest, and provost guards were instituted to keep a watch over the six regiments posted in Greenville, but the story faded from public interest and into history. And within a few weeks, Weaver Smith was forgotten.

A VERY ODD FELLOW

Newspapers shied away from using the words *rape* and *abortion* in 1912, but that is what Thurston Vaughn was accused of while he was an employee of the Odd Fellows Orphanage, and that is what the papers reported.

The Odd Fellows were a fraternal organization that claimed to "improve and elevate the character of mankind"; they ran the orphanage in Greenville on Tanglewood Drive, which operated for about twenty years before closing in 1926 due to numerous tales of abuses.

Thurston U. Vaughn was chosen by the Odd Fellows to be the orphanage superintendent. At twenty-six years of age, Vaughn was working as a teacher at Locust Hill School in Tigerville and attending classes at Furman University. He lived with his wife, Ella Neves Vaughn, and their daughter, Ruth. Vaughn was described as very small in stature and exceedingly manipulative. In May 1912, an eighteen-year-old woman who had since left the orphanage came forward with her story that she had been repeatedly raped by Vaughn and that he even performed an abortion on her. Four others soon came forward and offered similar accounts to the Odd Fellows Board of Trustees. Vaughn had left the orphanage, too; he had resigned in January and was working for an insurance company while living in an "elegant" newly purchased home. The board conducted an internal investigation, and a warrant was executed by Sheriff J. Perry Poole.

News of the young man's exploits for "unmentionable offenses" soon spread throughout the shocked community, as Vaughn had been regarded as a prominent Christian citizen. The hunt for Vaughn continued for several days. During a search of his house, deputies came across Vaughn's brother, who claimed he had gone "north," but he was caught a few days later while attempting to flee Greenville in a car and was arrested. He protested his innocence and asked that the public "suspend judgement" until they learn the truth. The *Pickens Sentinel*, on June 6, 1912, creatively described the awful crimes:

> *He is not only charged with criminal assault upon the person of a girl under 14 years of age but is accused of living in adultery with her and administering to her certain treatment which brought about relief from the embarrassing physical condition in which she found herself.*

Vaughn threatened to write an exposé on the Odd Fellows, which was then in damage control mode, pleading with its brethren to remain silent. The Odd Fellows also obtained defense counsel for Vaughn, employing the firm Martin & Blythe.

By June, Vaughn had sawed his way to freedom, escaping his jail cell by allegedly hacking through a bar with a saw. Jailers speculated that he must have had help from the outside, with papers reporting that his brother had recently purchased a hacksaw and blades. News of Vaughn mortgaging his home to the tune of $4,000 were also being reported, and authorities feared that Vaughn had the means to be on the run for a while. It wasn't until September that Vaughn was caught in Baltimore. A young Greenvillian, R.E. Allen Jr., had recently accepted a job at a bank there, recognized Vaughn in church and called the police. Vaughn had been teaching Sunday school and had enrolled in medical school without worry. When detectives arrived at the church, they said, "Hello, Vaughn. What are you doing in Baltimore?" Vaughn panicked and looked for an escape, but he was had. During a search of his wallet, several clippings from the *Greenville News* regarding his exploits and about $450 were found. Back in custody, authorities questioned Vaughn about who had helped him get out of the jail, and he gave a curious answer, stating that he had "lots of friends in Greenville" who were willing to spend money to see that he was freed.

Greenville sheriff J. Perry Poole arrived in Baltimore to return Vaughn to South Carolina. Having perhaps a moment of clarity, Vaughn broke down and confessed all, telling Poole that he was guilty of the charges against him. He claimed he had been tempted by the Devil and cried about what he had done to his wife and daughter, saying, "It is breaking my heart to think what my child will have to face as she grows older." While leaving the Baltimore lock-up on the arm of Sheriff Poole, Vaughn gave a statement to the newspaper men gathered outside: "I regret it all—regret it all. If only it could be undone." The reporters noted that "pathos marked every faltering utterance of a broken man." Vaughn was placed in the state penitentiary in Columbia for safe keeping.

The sensational trial of Vaughn began on October 21. Prior to the criminal trial, Etta Jackson, the victim in this case, filed a civil suit against Vaughn for $10,000. A line of questioning into this matter allegedly drove the courtroom to theatrics when defense attorney B.F. Martin of Martin & Blythe threw punches at prosecuting attorney John McSwain. The melee went on for several minutes while the courtroom spectators were in hysterics. A half dozen officers attempted to separate the two men. Judge Purdy slammed down his gavel several times and threatened that the next man to cause an outburst was going to jail. Sheriff Poole and a few other officers managed to finally pull them apart. Martin was taken into the hallway, bleeding profusely, while McSwain appeared unscathed. The crowd in the courtroom, including Vaughn's wife and daughter, nearly erupted into a riot, but Judge Purdy was able to maintain order. Once quiet was restored, the court recessed for a lunch break and returned in the afternoon to a closed session, where looky-loos were kept at bay. The next afternoon, without his family in attendance, Vaughn faced the jury and stated his testimony as recorded by the *Columbia Record* on October 28, 1912:

Gentlemen, it is useless to say that in this instance I am greatly humiliated, and for months and months I have had agonizing hours over the whole matter. I wish to say this in the outset: that I have never wished to conceal one whit of the truth when the time came to make a clear statement. I have been so cautious in these particulars that some have inferred that I had denied my guilt. I know that some have had that impression, but I knew that I was guilty and would tell it at the proper time. For that reason, I have made impressions that were unfavorable to me. I want to say here and now that I am going to take full responsibility. I want to take it off of that girl. I want to say that I have loved the girl always, but that love has been misdirected and misused. I don't think the girl will deny today the reality of my love in many respects, yet my conduct towards her would make her take the position towards me which she now takes and justly takes.

As superintendent of the orphanage, I had entire control of her. I realize that now. I did it under circumstances about which I would not care to go into details here. At the very point I thought myself the strongest, I found myself the weakest. I found that the Devil had attacked me with a more subtle and powerful temptation in the very place I thought I could not be tempted. I cannot now go into the details of the circumstances surrounding me when I fell, and I now assume full responsibility and ask God to save that girl.

Now, as to the treatment of the children out there; of course, I whipped them, but I never did wish to be cruel. I did not abuse them and had no desire to do so. But as hellish as this weight of sin has been, and despite the suffering of my body and soul, it has brought an entirely new viewpoint of life. I am not speaking it to make my position clear, and of this for sympathy, I am simply stat—I want to say this: that if it took all of this to save, to bring me to where I stand, and in spite of all of this, to redeem my soul and save me from Hell, I am thankful for it today.

I now have a better conception of God and man. With that fact in view, realizing the cheapness of life. I can be of better service to God and to man. I feel that if you will give me another opportunity, after pleading guilty to this charge, and let me have another chance, I can be of more service to God than ever before. I feel that I can live a life of sublime service and consecration to God. As dark as it may seem, as disgusting as it may seem to you, as hellish as it appears, I feel that in the depths of my heart I can go forward in better service, and I make this plea to you.

What is life? It is a very small thing. It is a very short time here, and my suffering it would soon be over, and I would be dead. Then it is a matter of eternity. But my present plea is that I have sinned, that I have suffered the tortures of the damned, that if I am given another opportunity, that the hold I now have on God, with the strength of the new faith I have in him, from out of this awful sin, I believe I can go out into the dives of sin in this state and be of service to my state and my God in reclaiming the evil-doers, in saving the state great expense and in redeeming them of their crimes and sins.

I believe truly that I can be of great service to my God and my fellow man. I love my life, it is true, but simply feel that in view of this new conception, life is a very small matter. Life is not eternal; it is a mere temporary existence. That which comes from God to God must return. So far as death is concerned, it is very small; it is the greater something which comes after.

During his testimony, some jurors audibly wept; tears even rolled down the cheeks of Judge Purdy. In closing, Vaughn requested that he be allowed to live, as he wanted to prove to his wife that he could be reformed. The jury took four minutes to return a verdict of guilty, and the judge sentenced Thurston Vaughn to the electric chair. His execution was set for December 20.

Despite the fisticuffs, tales of woe and courtroom tears, this case was far from over. Vaughn had more to say. As he was being led back to the state penitentiary in Columbia, Vaughn made another confession, this time to Sheriff J. Perry Poole, Deputy Sheriff Hunsinger and the new sheriff-elect Hendrix Rector. The *Greenville News* described how Vaughn managed to escape from jail in June: "He said that his brother gave Jailer Phillips $10 to transfer T.U. Vaughn from the main cells to a cell used for women, which has a barred window opening on the jail yard." Vaughn said the night before his escape, Constable Reuben Gosnell came to the cell window and tried to saw the bars but was unable to do it and went away. The next night, former sheriff Jeff Gilreath came and successfully sawed through the bars and then handed the saw to Vaughn. Vaughn swore that he would "sit in the electric chair itself and make the same confession as to who helped him escape." Governor Cole Blease immediately swore out warrants for those "aiding a prisoner to escape" and the ex-sheriff, constable and Policeman Alex Phillips were arrested and paraded "through the streets of Greenville."

The *Keowee Courier* of Pickens reported that the accused sat in jail for about an hour before "five substantial businessmen, commanding more than a million dollars cash," arrived to sign bonds. A circus-like atmosphere had taken up in the streets outside the jail when the men were released. Most of the citizenry believed that political animosity was at the root of the arrests, as Gilreath had been in a race for sheriff against Poole and Rector.

Gilreath sent a wire to Governor Blease, demanding to know if the governor had ordered his arrest. It all played out in the papers like a penny dreadful, with Blease beginning to backtrack, stating that he had left the matter for Sheriff-Elect Rector and Solicitor Bonham to decide based on the evidence. Some of the evidence that came to light was the fact that Vaughn had boarded at the home of Gilreath's father, Perry Duncan Gilreath, during his time at Furman and that Jeff Gilreath and Vaughn were close friends. The jailer also swore in an affidavit that he had seen Gilreath assisting Vaughn to escape. Gilreath said that the accusations were untrue. "If Vaughn ever ate a meal at my father's house, I do not know it. I will say that my father assisted Vaughn and other poor boys of the community to obtain an education. It was a custom of my father to lend his assistance to any bright, energetic and deserving boy of the neighborhood who desired an education." The allegation that he sprung Vaughn loose was also discredited. "That I liberated Vaughn in order to defeat Sheriff Poole, that is beneath notice. I would like to say, however, that Mr. Rector was also a candidate for sheriff at the same time and the same motive could be charged to him." The warrants against all three, Gilreath, Reuben Gosnell and Alex Phillips, were withdrawn, and Blease suddenly went mum on the entire ordeal.

Meanwhile, Vaughn's lawyers hatched an appeal, with the supreme court granting him a stay. The ire of the *Greenville News* was palpable, as it wrote, "There is need for very little speculation as to why the people resort so often to lynching." Vaughn was moved from death row to the main prison building at the state penitentiary to await a hearing scheduled for February 1913. Details of the appeal included the fact that Vaughn was sentenced to the electric chair when hanging was the supposed punishment for such a crime and that Vaughn's confession was misconstrued. Legally, they argued that he had confessed to a great moral wrong and not to rape, per se. By July, the supreme court ruled that the Greenville court's verdict would stand, and that Vaughn would face death. Vaughn's lawyers would not give up the fight and were prepared to fight in the U.S. Supreme Court.

Vaughn was not out of cards to play, although he likely didn't have a full deck. In late 1914, reports began to surface that he was going insane. Even Sheriff Rector stated that the guy was nuts. He was transferred to the state hospital, where he would constantly pick at his hair and clothes as though they were infested with bugs. A board of examiners was called up to decide if Vaughn was insane or pretending in order to avoid the electric chair. Doctors bickered back and forth before reaching the conclusion that Vaughn was mentally incompetent and theorized that he might never have been at any point in his life due to an abnormal contour of his head. This dragged out for two years, and by the end of 1916, Vaughn was confined to an asylum, having supposedly not uttered a word in that time.

Almost three years went by, and Vaughn all but disappeared from the news and the public consciousness. But all the while, he was sweet-talking a nurse, and the loony lothario was on the run again in September 1919. Vaughn was supposed to have been transported to Greenville for some sanity tests when a dummy constructed of fabric and stuffed clothes was discovered in his bed, and a set of keys was reported missing. Vaughn merely walked out of the asylum's front doors. A nurse named Sandal Beamguard left her job at the hospital six months later to join Vaughn in Tampa, Florida, where they were married. Vaughn lived under the assumed name T.E. Earl and was a teacher for Port Tampa Schools until authorities finally caught up with him in April 1921. At this point, the case had dragged on for nine years. Before being separated from Vaughn, his wife allegedly said to him, "Goodbye, dear. I'll see you in heaven." Vaughn continued to maintain that he was in fact T.E. Earl and that he never went by another name or had a former wife in Greenville. When he was told that the former Miss Beamguard had given up her husband, Vaughn insisted that they were just "scheming" to set him up in a trap. Vaughn was placed in a straitjacket and a padded cell to await extradition, and then he was strangely placed in a cell on "murderers' row" with three other inmates. On shaving day, it was alleged that Vaughn took the straight razor and sliced his own throat. Physicians confirmed the powerful stroke was self-inflicted. Authorities were eager to charge Sandal Earl (Vaughn) in his escape but lacked evidence, and she was never charged. She claimed that Vaughn would not tell her who provided the keys but was adamant that it was not her. Vaughn's remains were returned to South Carolina and interred at the State Hospital Cemetery, according to the wishes of his father.

Ella Neves, the original Mrs. Vaughn, returned to her maiden name and seemingly lived a normal life, remaining in Greenville until she died in 1965. Their daughter, Ruth, who went by Ruth Neves and later became Ruth Pollard, worked for the *Greenville News* for several years. She died in 1990 and was buried beside her mother in the Mush Creek Baptist Church Cemetery in Travelers Rest.

THE MOTHER-IN-LAW MURDER

A warm June evening that was made to be enjoyed in 1919 turned to chaos, as bullets struck a mother and daughter while they relaxed on their porch. Loud pops were heard coming from the gun held by Hugh Bramlett, the estranged husband of Cora McHugh. Bullets hit Mrs. Lou Caroline McHugh, Cora's mother, and her sister, Peola. As the former fireman sped off in his Ford sedan, Mrs. McHugh clung to life, and Peola screamed, alerting her sister, who was inside.

While Mrs. McHugh was rushed to the hospital, not expected to make it, officers pursued Bramlett. They found him at his home nine miles outside of the city. He resisted arrest, telling officers to "go to hell," and was shot with a shotgun before being brought to the county jail by Sheriff Hendrix Rector. Unlike that of Mrs. McHugh, his condition was not serious.

Bramlett had been in trouble before; a year earlier, he was charged with assault in connection with his domestic situation. He had been arrested for threatening to shoot his wife and her mother, but they had disarmed him, and he had been released on good behavior. The unrest had recently culminated in Cora moving out of their home and into her mother's home with their two children, Virginia (six) and Hugh Jr. (three). Cora had feared Bramlett's increased paranoia and general instability. Those fears materialized when McHugh died from her injuries, as one of the bullets had penetrated her intestines.

At the hospital, Cora told the police that Bramlett had carried a grudge toward her mother, and it had been very painful for the family, but she could offer no specific reason as to why he had shot at her. An eyewitness, an employee at Cureton's Bakery named Mr. J.P. Gosa, was sitting on the curb across the street from the McHugh home when he heard the initial shots. He explained that after three shots, Bramlett turned with his pistol in hand and then went back to fire again. As the ladies screamed and fell, Gosa looked around for help, and by the time he looked in Bramlett's direction again, he was gone.

As Peola recovered from her wounds, the law firm Bonham & Price was secured to prosecute Bramlett. Fearing that a mob would come to deal with the matter, Bramlett was removed to the state penitentiary, where he waited to be tried for murder.

Robert Martin of Martin & Blythe would represent Bramlett, who began the trial by entering a plea of insanity and planned to show that Bramlett had not been in his right mind at the time of the shootings. The highlight of the case came when Peola, dressed all in black, hobbled to the stand on crutches to recount the evening she and her mother had been shot. She reported that Bramlett had jumped out of his car, and when she saw him, she moved to go into the house. He yelled out, "Stop, God damn you! I have got you. I will kill you this time." As he fired at her and "Mamma," Mrs. McHugh tried to rush her daughter into the house. They were shot at again, causing McHugh to fall in the doorway. He started down the steps, and Peola thought he was gone, but then he turned and fired once more before fleeing in his automobile. She also recounted that Bramlett had come to the home in May on an "unfriendly mission"; he had arrived drunk, brandishing a gun and threatening to "kill her mother." She explained that Bramlett would have "wild spells" and that her mother had forbidden him from coming to the house after the incident in May. She said that Bramlett and her sister had been married for about seven years and that he had gotten along well with the family until he took up drinking about three years prior. She stated that Bramlett had gone to a hospital in North Carolina to be treated for alcoholism in 1917.

Chief of Police Noe testified that he was at the arrest when Bramlett resisted and was ultimately brought into custody. He had not smelled liquor on the defendant and did not think he had been under the influence. Noe went on to state that he had known Bramlett for thirteen years and that in the last three, "there had come a great change in him." When he had been arrested for the assault on Mrs. McHugh the year before, he had tried to "break up his cell" and had bit one of the officers. That time, he had pled guilty and promised the court to give up whiskey. Noe did not think he showed signs of insanity.

Solicitor Martin read an affidavit from eighty-one-year-old Mary Garrison, who stated it was her opinion that insanity ran in the Bramlett family, as she had been acquainted with a relative, William Bramlett, whom everyone regarded as insane, "though not violently so." William had committed suicide, as had his brother Walter. A third brother, Zeph, had left home and was also thought to have been dead by his own hand.

Bramlett was on the stand for almost the entirety of the next day. He felt that killing Mrs. McHugh had been justified, because "they had wrecked my home, wrecked my life." He had intended to go there to "get my wife and children, to kill or get killed." He admitted to alcoholism but said he believed he could have worked things out with Cora had it not been for the constant meddling of her family. He explained that their problems had begun in 1915, after the death of their second baby. Cora had been ill and was being seen by Dr. Furman in their home. Mrs. McHugh and Peola came and took charge, demanding that Cora be moved to the lower floor of the house. Not wanting to create hard feelings, Bramlett allowed his wife to be moved, and soon after, she contracted pneumonia. The baby was born the next day but did not survive. After that, their relationships became strained, and McHugh repeatedly told him that "they was going to take her away from me; she should not live with me." He claimed that she humiliated him and "caused unpleasantness in my home all the time." He soon took to alcohol to calm his nerves and began to drink "all the time," noting that soon, he could not do without it. Following an argument with Cora, he checked himself into a hospital in Morganton, North Carolina, which he said was a hospital for the insane. After eighteen days, he returned home to his family, and things seemed fine for a couple of weeks, until an argument over money resulted in Bramlett slapping Cora, striking her for the first time. He was so remorseful that they made up within minutes, but when he returned from work later that day, Mrs. McHugh was there to raise Cain, following Bramlett all over the house and calling him a brute. Bramlett threatened to have the police called to remove McHugh, to which she replied, "If you do, you will be sorry for it." The next day, Cora's brothers, Palmer and Pierce, arrived to rattle

Bramlett's cage and belittle him over his drinking. At this point, Bramlett broke down in tears on the stand, telling the court how much he loved his wife and how he had done everything he could for her. She was even a part of a business he was starting with his brother. As for the previous assault, he charged that after some words, he had hit his wife, and McHugh came after him with a shovel. He then took it from her and struck her with it. He gave himself up the next day, and when he got out of jail and went home to find Cora and the children, it was his idea that they leave the house for a while so that he could recover. That was the last time they lived together as a family. Lately, they had talked about getting back together and moving to North Carolina to get a fresh start, "but she could not get away from her people."

The day he shot Mrs. McHugh and Peola, Bramlett said that he had phoned the house to talk to his wife, but his mother-in-law had refused to let him speak to her, telling him that if he did not stay away, he would be "a dead man." He recounted that the two were conspiring to turn his children against him. He had seen Peola and his kids on the street several times, and the kids would wave and say, "Hello, Daddy." But Peola would not let them go to him and would make them hang their heads down. Bramlett was asked by his counsel why he had gone to the McHugh house, to which he replied that he had gone to get his wife and kids. Through sobs, he stated that he "wanted my children taken out of bondage of hatred for me—wanted them taken out of bondage." He had planned to collect his family to take them to his mother's house in Fayetteville, North Carolina. He said he did not go there with the intention of shooting anyone, but in a haze, he had opened fire when he saw them on the porch.

During cross-examination, Bramlett was asked if he thought he was insane, but he said that he had not decided if he was and that was going to leave that for the courts and doctors to determine.

The day's session ended with the testimony of J.D. Bridges, who had worked with Bramlett on contracting jobs and had known him for ten years. He said that Bramlett had come to him in 1917, very distressed over his situation at home, and he said that he seemed to be in "mortal pain." Bridges described his friend as being "exceptionally bright at times and exceptionally crazy at times." His drinking would cause spells, and Bramlett would become "the craziest man I ever saw when mad."

The third day of the trial brought out the stagecraft of Mrs. Lou Bramlett, Bramlett's mother, who had to be assisted to the stand, where she answered every question with great difficulty. She related the family tree, explaining to the court that Bramlett's descendants were insane on both his maternal and paternal sides. Every skeleton in his closet—uncles, cousins, second cousins and even a great-great-uncle—was exposed to the jury. Suicide seemed to be the highest cause of death in his lineage, starting with his father. She described her son as being a "nervous, high-strung" boy but that he had a kind heart and was well liked in the community while he was growing up. In the last three years, she had considered her son "to be of unsound mind." Her testimony ended when she collapsed and was taken to the judge's chambers to be attended to by a doctor.

Other character witnesses offered similar tales of Bramlett coming undone in the last three years or so, and that his drinking alcohol would turn to violence. His brother Frank told the court that they had had plans for their own business, but that Bramlett had become unable to carry on his own affairs and was fixated on his domestic troubles. He considered his brother "a regular liquor head" but said that things were worse as he was coming off the alcohol and didn't think the whiskey was totally "responsible for his change." His family had tried to encourage Bramlett to quit drinking.

After a thorough analysis of Bramlett's ancestry and physical examinations, Dr. J.W. Babcock diagnosed Bramlett with a "typical history of paranoia." The former superintendent of the state asylum believed, "The act was the outcome of the diseased condition of his mind, and I have no doubt whatever but that he was insane when the act was committed." Babcock continued, "I do not believe at the time of the act that he could judge the legal or moral wrong of the homicide."

Eight days after the trial began, the jurors took an hour and a half to reach a verdict of guilty, and Bramlett was sentenced to the electric chair by Judge James Peurifoy. After reading the verdict, Bramlett's counsel advised the judge that they would seek a new trial. Bramlett showed little emotion as he was ushered out of the courtroom and returned to jail to await his electrocution, which was scheduled for October 17, 1919.

The early 1900s saw mental illness as a stigma, and it was usually written off as hysteria. Severe cases were deposited in "insane asylums," where treatment was more like a type of punishment and uses of lobotomies, electroshock treatment and isolation were the norm.

Dr. Babcock reasoned that Bramlett drank excessively due to his psychosis and paranoia. In all his meetings with Bramlett, he observed that he was "controlled by one central fixed idea": that "the McHugh family had persecuted him and driven him to the extremity of attacking the two of them." Babcock further declared that his analysis of Bramlett was as "distinct and clear-cut insanity as found in the books," continuing to say that Bramlett would not have had any indication between "legal and moral wrong" during his act. He concluded by stating that "the defendant went to the McHugh home under an insane delusion that rendered him incapable of understanding what he did."

Bramlett's appeal awarded him a stay of execution. From the Greenville County Jail, he filed for a petition, asking to see his two young children. In it, he wrote that he believed Cora was willing to let the children visit him, but Peola was still wielding her influence and would disallow her sister and the children to see him. He asked that the judge mandate such an order. Cora's attorney, James Price, requested that the order be held until the supreme court case was settled, but a few days later, she surprised Bramlett with a family reunion at the jail. The *Greenville News* noted that the voluntary visit came as a shock to her attorneys. The jailor allowed them about two hours in a private parlor that was supervised by the sheriff for the bittersweet get-together.

In July 1920, Bramlett was granted a new trial, which was to begin in November. But when the court was unable to obtain a full jury of twelve men, a mistrial was declared by Judge J.W. DeVore.

The third trial began in January 1921, and it put Bramlett on the stand for three hours. Other witnesses from the first trial were introduced to the jury, and they recommended mercy with a sentence of life in prison. Bramlett told reporters that he was ready to go to the penitentiary but wanted to see his babies, stating that he was "a sick man." He was remanded to the chain gang for hard labor.

After Bramlett served seven years in prison, Governor Richards granted him clemency based on numerous petitions from family members and Bramlett's good behavior. McHugh's owns sons did not object, and Cora lobbied on behalf of her husband. She also wrote to Richards, saying that "this unfortunate circumstance arose by reason of domestic misunderstanding and interferences." The growing children also wrote letters in support of their father's freedom.

The *State* newspaper in Columbia reported that the Bramletts were living a "quiet life" in March 1930, which is supported by the U.S. Census for that year, which shows the family unit lived together on a farm in Oconee. However, by 1933, the union appears to have been undone, as Bramlett was charged and convicted of nonsupport. The 1940 census shows Cora was a divorced proprietor of a "tourist home" in Charlotte, North Carolina, while it seems Bramlett dropped off the map.

When he resurfaced in May 1942, it was because he was arrested and booked for public drunkenness. Hugh T. Bramlett was found dangling in his cell, where he hanged himself with his own belt. Despite his second chance at life, his demons had finally won out.

A TALE OF THREE SHERIFFS

You can leave the Dark Corner, but the Dark Corner won't leave you. Hendrix Rector was determined to make something of himself. He was the fifth of seven children, born in 1882 to John William Rector and Rebecca Barton in Glassy Mountain Township. The Rectors settled in that part of Greenville in the early 1800s, when Hendrix's great-grandfather Reverend Lewis Rector moved there from Virginia. The reverend was one of the founding members of the Brushy Creek Baptist Church and was buried in an old Rector family cemetery, which now stands on the property of the fire station on Blacks Drive.

Hendrix was fourteen years old when his father died. He worked his way through North Greenville Academy and was hired as part of the Greenville Police force. He had a reputation of being a "by-the-book" lawman and was also regarded as fearless when it came to capturing moonshiners and destroying distilleries.

In January 1912, Rector quit the police department to go into real estate, but by February, he had announced he was running for sheriff against incumbent J. Perry Poole. The *Greenville News* lauded the decision on February 7, 1912, writing: "No member of the department was ever held in higher regard by the general public than Mr. Rector, and there was genuine regret on the part of the law-abiding citizens of Greenville when he severed his connection with the police department." The paper noted that the remarks were not to advance Rector's candidacy but that they were "statements of facts." Former sheriff Jeff D. Gilreath soon entered the race as well. By September, it had come down to a runoff between Gilreath and Rector, described by the papers as the fiercest political fight ever seen in the county. Gilreath had formerly been the sheriff for eight years and campaigned on being anti–Governor Blease. Meanwhile, Rector was described as an "avowed Blease man." Coleman Blease was a follower of Benjamin Tillman, the former anti–civil rights governor. Blease was a champion of the mill workers and against any progressive "welfare" programs, including mandating school for children. He also complained about women's groups, calling their members "busybodies" who should be home in the kitchen. He was well known for having an abusive and disparaging attitude.

Gilreath was serving as a member of the police commission and was tenured there when Rector quit the force, and tension between the two men was at an all-time high. On September 12, Rector was declared the winner of the election with a majority of sixteen votes. He was nominated by executive committee, with Gilreath threatening to contest, citing irregularities at the polls. Then came that bizarre incident during the Thurston Vaughn case, in which Gilreath, Reuben Gosnell and Policeman Alex Phillips were arrested and accused of springing Vaughn loose from the jail. Early reports stated that Governor Blease had ordered the warrants, but after anger ensued from Greenville's upper crust, Blease demurred, throwing his sheriff-elect under the bus and laying the blame at his feet. The matter quickly went away, and the charges were dropped, but Gilreath was mad. He told the papers that "there was personal animosity at the bottom of this outrageous matter." He complained that Rector had locked him up and then didn't even bother to show up at the hearing.

Days later, a large gathering of mill operatives, merchants, bankers and brokers announced their endorsement of an independent candidate for sheriff. W.F. Verdin was put forth as a candidate, as Rector was then deemed in "bad repute." This was no longer about politics—it was a matter of "simple manhood and decency." The hit pieces against Rector were released immediately, with the first printed in the November 4, 1912 issue of the *Greenville News*. It was addressed to "whom it may concern." A man named J.F. Alexander, in two very lengthy paragraphs, laid out that he had been "worried by Hendrix Rector and his crowd." He wrote that he was forced by Rector to perjure himself when signing an affidavit and that he was just "a strange boy in a strange land, without friends or money." He went on to describe his fear about being put in prison if Rector was in charge, "shut off from the outside world." He was under such "mental strain and fright," he didn't know what he had signed.

Rector was victorious over Verdin, even though eleven ballot boxes turned up "missing," and he was sworn in in January 1913. The colorful character soon assumed the tasks of the Greenville sheriff: arresting moonshiners and gamblers, solving missing persons cases, witnessing marriages, maintaining order at the county jail and living up to campaign promises of reform, often in the company of his bloodhound Jack. In September, he revoked the commission of the deputy sheriff, J.W. Goldsmith in Piedmont, stating

Hendrix Rector (*left*) in his office with an unidentified man. *Courtesy of the Greenville County Library.*

that he was informed Goldsmith took every opportunity to knock his office and that he knew Goldsmith had worked tirelessly for Verdin's campaign and didn't consider him "worthy to hold office under me." The Piedmont Manufacturing Company took issue with this and went before a judge to say that it had selected Deputy Sheriff Goldsmith and was paying his salary. The company also said that Rector's decision was based on criticism of his administration. It argued that since Goldsmith was appointed on its recommendation, an executive officer would have a say in his dismissal, not Sheriff Rector. After several weeks, the judge concluded that Rector was within his rights to dismiss Goldsmith. Rector had won another battle and was about to declare war.

In early 1914, Rector and his deputies conducted regular raids on "blind tigers" (illicit drinking and gambling establishments). Whiskey and beer were seized by the gallon, and arrests were made several nights a week. Rector vowed to carry on until these speakeasys were closed and the trade of alcohol was "stamped out" in Greenville. He announced:

The illicit sale of whiskey has existed in Greenville County now for many years, but the end is in sight, partly so at least. Considering the fact that we have a prohibition county, I want this law enforced and intend to see that it is, so far as much as possible. I want it understood that I will deal with all classes alike, handling the wealthy clubman in the same manner as the small "tiger."

A regular deputy who accompanied Rector on his crusades was Jake Gosnell, a cousin of Reuben Gosnell, the constable who had been arrested with Jeff Gilreath during the Thurston Vaughn escape.

On February 17, 1914, the *Herald* of Rock Hill reported that the odor of booze was permeating the air as Rector and his team conducted a "pouring-out day." The storage of beer and whiskey at the courthouse had become so great that they had to dump large quantities of alcohol into the sewer.

In July 1914, Rector's deputy Jake Gosnell was put on trial for throwing a small dog from a platform at city park during an event in which senate candidates were speaking. Rector spoke on his behalf, telling the court that Gosnell did not "intentionally ill-treat the dog" but that he would plead guilty. Gosnell was fined five dollars for the unfortunate event. In September, Rector was forced to arrest his deputy, as Gosnell was involved in a fight at the courthouse, in which he punched a man in the nose over a heated political discussion. When asked about the incident, Rector stated that Gosnell was not a deputy sheriff at all but worked for him occasionally as a bailiff and as his driver. In December, the *Greenville News* described Jake Gosnell as "deputy" when detailing an arrest made by him and Rector in which he shot the accused. Gosnell's .38-caliber bullet tore through the victim's foot, but the wound was not considered serious.

The end of 1914 culminated with a terrible automobile wreck that occurred while Rector was driving and swerved to miss a dog. Rector and three other passengers were thrown from the "machine." Rector's injuries were reportedly grim, but after convalescing for several weeks, he was back on the job, enforcing liquor laws. In April 1915, the *Greenville News* asked, "When Is a Deputy Sheriff Not One? If Not, Why Not?" This headline was accompanied by an article about Jake Gosnell being fined for speeding. The account went on to describe Gosnell doing work for the sheriff's office for over a year. Rector was summoned to the court and again described Gosnell as a bailiff at the court, not a deputy sheriff. The article opined of the "complicated condition," as Gosnell made many arrests for the department. A few days later, Rector spoke out over the confusion, stating that he had only two deputies who worked for him, but from time to time, he deputized men to serve warrants, pointing out that once that work was complete, those men were no longer considered officers. To make matters worse, the legislative delegation of South Carolina, in an unprecedented move, voted to remove the county jail from under Rector's watch at the sheriff's department, thus decreasing his salary. Jake Gosnell went on to become a special agent for the Internal Revenue Service.

In August, Rector made the news for getting into a fistfight with the postmaster in a barbershop. While Rector sat in a chair, reading the paper, Postmaster Dave Traxler came over, and some heated words were exchanged. Rector repeatedly told Traxler he didn't want any trouble, but when Traxler continued, they came to blows. Both men were fined, and Rector gave a statement to the paper, laying the blame at the feet of his old enemy Jeff Gilreath and accusing Traxler of being one of his acolytes. He wrote that they had tried ever since he entered office to engage in "some rash act." Rector described giving Traxler three chances to go away and said that he was not at fault for what had taken place and that he had tried to avoid it. The *Watchman and Southron* of August 14, 1915, blamed the fisticuffs on "bitter factionalism." Rector claimed that the rural police were "fighting him all the time" and that he was constantly followed by detectives. He told the press that he "would kill the next man who came at him, if it means my electrocution in ten minutes."

In May 1916, following an announcement that he was going to run for sheriff again, Rector vowed that he would not be silenced by his political enemies. His determination, probably motivated more out of spite than longing to continue as sheriff, referred to his opposition as "old, run-down vagrants." Other candidates appeared to come out of the woodwork from all over the county, publishing their manifestos in the papers. Rector's manifesto took up three-quarters of a page in the July 2, 1916 issue of the *Greenville News*, highlighting his accomplishments while stressing that since day one, he had to fight for his very existence. He pleaded with the people of Greenville to give him a chance at vindication, to "serve them free from any interference."

On an early morning in August, Rector telephoned the newspaper to tell it that he had been fired on twice on his way home. Both shots fired toward him went astray, with one hitting his car. Rector explained that although it was dark, he could see a man plainly, and he returned fire, possibly striking his assailant, but the man ran away as he started to chase him down an embankment. Two days later, Rector arrested two men he believed were involved in the shooting, John McCracken and Ed Turner. Earlier in the week, a warrant had been sworn out against McCracken for posting an obscene poem and pictures about Rector on a store door. With the poem described as "unfit for decent people to read," McCracken was also wanted for storing whiskey. McCracken, a local weirdo who lived in a house on Endel Street surrounded by barricades, including a board plastered out front that read "Behind this fence, a lunatic lives, and his name is Legion," was later released along with Turner, as there was no solid evidence they had fired at the sheriff.

Rector won his reelection and threw a huge celebratory barbecue, inviting everybody, even those who had voted against him. "I am going to be everybody's sheriff. I have buried the hatchet and am willing to smoke the pipe of peace with all my enemies." The railroads gave out half-priced fares so people from Greenville, Spartanburg, Anderson, Union, Pickens and Greenwood Counties could attend the barbecue. Former governor Cole Blease and other notables were in attendance to address the crowd of about ten thousand. The sheriff's fresh start quickly resumed business as usual, as he filled the jail docket after a "sweeping raid in Cripple Creek." Rector and his men stormed local "hash joints" in what was described as a "cyclone hitting the place." He also worked closely with the rural police when a Mrs. L.C. Jarnigan was killed in a hit-and-run automobile accident in October 1916 on her way home from church. Rector offered up a reward of $100 for information leading to an arrest in the case. Rector worked leads for several weeks before finally arresting three men and a woman; the driver had been drinking heavily at the time of the accident. The papers acknowledged Rector's clever detective skills in the case, and calls went up for a state law to bond drivers.

In February 1917, the thirty-four-year-old Rector became seriously ill with la grippe, a severe flu. He convalesced at home with care from his wife and was back at work in a week. News of Reuben Gosnell's reelection to chief of the rural police was making rounds in the papers. Rector commented that he didn't care who the chief was but that he wanted a say in who would be jailer, because he needed someone to work in harmony with him. He appealed to the Charities and Correction Commission, but the legislature was unwilling to relinquish its power grab.

In March, Rector's brother Carlos was appointed special agent of the Internal Revenue Service with headquarters in Greenville, occupying a vacancy made by the end of Jake Gosnell's term. Rector petitioned the state to establish the Rector Detective Agency, which Carlos would manage, and it was approved. Gosnell was brought before a judge with a charge of contempt of court regarding a dispute that had taken place a few days prior in a crowded courtroom. Rector had ordered a side door of the courthouse closed when Gosnell tried to get out and was stopped. He caused a scene, shouting that the sheriff "didn't have a damned thing to do with it" and referring to Rector as a "crook." On cross-examination, Rector testified that he and Gosnell had some words that week over some money Gosnell had collected and allegedly not returned. The judge ruled to give Gosnell the benefit of the doubt, since the disturbance was minor, and they dismissed any charges of disorderly conduct. The public bickering between the two men continued when an open letter from Gosnell to Rector appeared in the *Greenville News* on September 15, 1917. It detailed the charges made when, two days prior, Rector had gone before the city council to admonish a report provided to the war department by a secret service investigator about a military camp in Greenville. Information was provided to the investigator by a "public service driver," and it detailed that Greenville had four hundred houses of "ill fame" and "numerous other instances of lawlessness." The report portrayed Greenville as "the worst city south of the Mason and Dixon line." Rector defended his town: "The statement is false and untrue in every way, and as sheriff of this county, I want council to take action in the matter. Greenville has fewer prostitutes and less lawlessness than it has ever had, and it's unfair that the good name of this city should be unjustly defamed." Rector had named the accused to the council, and the paper did not publish the name of the informant, but Gosnell outed himself with his public letter.

Sheriff Rector rang in 1918 by thanking the people of Greenville for their cooperation during 1917, saying that the year had been the city's best that he had known in terms of law enforcement. A resolution was drafted by the sheriff's association, endorsing Rector's control of the Grenville Jail. Rector used the *Greenville News*, which he both despised and used to his advantage interchangeably, to point out how much more taxpayers were shelling out for the prison to be under the control of a separate office as opposed to being entrusted to the sheriff's office. Alleging on January 31, 1918, "gross official corruption" in the county, Rector announced his intention to run for the House of Representatives the following summer, though his term for sheriff wouldn't expire for another two years. Supervising Auditor William Nolley Cruikshank was swift to rebut the reports of exuberant costs to the taxpayers and invited anyone interested to come examine the books for themselves. The *Greenville News* took this opportunity to run Cruikshank's reply on February 4, 1918, alongside an editorial describing Rector's desire to expose corruption at the county level. The editorial claimed that if Rector could do it, "he will be a big man and a Patriot"; however, if he failed to prove his claims, he would deserve to "be thoroughly discredited." The State Democratic Convention lambasted Rector for his announcement to run for the House of Representatives while he was sheriff and pointed out it would be against the rules for him to make campaign speeches at official venues in his capacity as sheriff. Rector seemed to be angering people in high places. The *Greenwood Journal* piped up with its own editorial, as relayed by the *Greenville News* on February 9. It accused Rector of using the press too much to blow his own horn:

> *The officer who is eternally writing articles for the newspapers and keeping himself before the public is the kind of fellow who does very little for the best interests of his country so far as restraining the lawlessness. People become disgusted, and when they see his name signed, be known that he is ready to wipe up some braggadocio article.*

Not one to sit by quietly, Rector had a humdinger of a reply, which was described as him "bellicosely flaying the naufrageous [an obscure term meaning 'in a state of danger or ruin/threatened'] press." In it, he explained that he only announced his candidacy to run for the House with one motive in mind: to expose the corruption of the "qualified electors of this county of the foul means employed by the kaiser (Cruikshank) of Greenville County's delegation" and that the people had a right to know. He accused them of using the newspapers to stir up "strife and criticism," referring to them as "rags" and "public panderers":

> *Now that my time has come to impose a blow for a cleaning up in our county politics, they should not object; they should heed the old adage "every dog has his day."…When we start to beat the rugs, let them get out of the house or breathe the dust.*

In June, Rector got one of his prayers answered when jailer W.R. Neeley resigned, giving notice to the Charities and Corrections Commission. While Neeley noted that his time as jailer had been "most pleasant," he stated that persons "holding official positions" had interfered with his duties. He also cited a recent charge of misconduct, of which he was fully exonerated.

In the summer, Rector claimed he had been bribed by former state senator John L. McLaurin to run for lieutenant governor. He claimed he was to receive $2,000 in cash if he was willing to run and support McLaurin for governor. Rector turned down the offer immediately and swore he would "tell a little more about it" if denials were made. He stated McLaurin had "lowered South Carolina politics to where it is beneath the notice of a gentleman." In a political meeting at Judson Mills, Rector explained that he had been approached by Victor Cheshire of the *Anderson Tribune*, who acted as an intermediary to facilitate the deal. Cheshire wrote a rebuttal, which was published in the *Greenville News* on July 7, 1918. He claimed that Rector was mistaken and wanted to know what he had been drinking that night. He had suggested that Rector run for lieutenant governor but said that he would save about $2,000 due to McLaurin's generosity while campaigning, paying for hotels and taking Rector with him in his touring car—it was not an upfront offer of cash. He also added that he hoped Rector would lose his bid for reelection, even though he admitted that he was the best sheriff Greenville County had ever had.

Rector did not run for the House of Representatives and probably had no reason to do so other than to rile up his opposition and to see what they would say and do. He threw his support behind former governor Cole Blease as he ran for state senate, participating in political rallies in the mill communities around town. He encouraged his followers to vote for Blease while using his platform to attack the chief of the rural police and foe Reuben Gosnell and to take swipes at the newly departed jailer Neeley. He also referred to *Anderson Tribune* editor Cheshire, who had recently come out against Blease, as a "law-breaker of various sorts," telling his audience to not pay attention to the newspaperman. The heavy campaigning did not win the seat for Blease, which was ultimately won by Nathaniel B. Dial.

As World War I dwindled to its close, Greenville was waging a war of its own, as the Spanish flu was raging through the city. Rector took to the paper to implore the city's citizens to take the disease seriously. The city and county were placed under quarantine, with schools, churches and public gathering places closed for about a month, but the threat of longer closures lingered. Thanksgiving was hampered by a heavy rain, which caused an unusual quiet for the sheriff's office. Rector noted that not even a single "crap game" was reported.

The year 1919 saw Greenville's number of influenza cases starting to subside, and it was back to business as usual for Rector and the sheriff's department. A visit to Briscoe's Garage on West Court Street led to a run-in with Jake Gosnell. Gosnell was having his car worked on when Rector walked in. Rector allegedly said, "Good morning, Jake," with Gosnell replying that

The vicinity of Briscoe's Garage on West Court Street, where Hendrix Rector was gunned down. *Photograph by John Stoy.*

he had no good morning for him. After a few words were exchanged back and forth, Gosnell fired his pistol four times, striking Rector down. All the service, good works, reform, political theater, muckraking and newspaper hijinks were dead—on the floor of Briscoe's Garage on the Fourth of July. Hendrix Rector was thirty-seven years old.

Gosnell was taken into custody at an undisclosed location, as mob violence was feared. Thousands of people reportedly showed up at the courthouse and jail as word of the murder spread throughout the town. Greenville was in mourning. Governor Cooper undertook the task of naming Rector's successor as Coroner Allison took intermediary charge of the sheriff's office.

The autopsy showed that Rector had been hit with four bullets, the first entering through his face. The second hit his right shoulder, the third struck his right-side ribs and the fourth hit his left lung and heart. The inquest revealed that years of animosity between the two over politics had come to a bitter end for Rector. He had not had the chance to pull his weapon and still had a cigarette in his left hand. Rector's pearl-handled revolver fell from his pocket as he was being lifted into the ambulance. Deputy Sheriff Bunyan

Keller, who was in the garage at the time of the incident, arrested Gosnell, who was taken to the state penitentiary for safekeeping. Gosnell's wife, Anna, had also been in the garage at the time of the gunfire.

The courtroom overflowed, and standing observers pushed out the doors for the inquest. Three of Rector's brothers, Carlos, James and Rome, were in attendance. His fourth brother, Jeff, was making his way home to Greenville, as he was serving in the U.S. Army and was stationed in New Jersey. Deputy Keller was the only witness to testify. He recounted that Gosnell had told his wife to get in the car and was going to get in the car himself when he was restrained, and Keller took charge of him. Mrs. Gosnell exclaimed, "Lord, have mercy! Jake, you oughtn't to have done that." The inquest jurors decided that Gosnell was to be tried for murder, and the trial was set for August.

Thousands turned out for the funeral at Graceland Cemetery, and it was called the largest "outpouring of citizens at any funeral ever held in the county." The procession from Rector's home on Laurens Road to the cemetery stretched on for over a mile. "Humanity lined the avenue leading from the entrance to the grave, a distance of over several hundred yards." Numerous fraternal organizations that Rector was a member of were represented, with the Woodmen of the World in charge of the service. Six sheriffs from outlying communities served as pallbearers. Evie, Rector's widow, fainted during the service, as she was having trouble getting air due to the dense crowds. The couple had an adopted son, Linwood, and he attended, along with Rector's elderly mother and her four remaining sons. The *Greenville News* offered an obituary that noted the bravery and outspokenness of a "man of the people," and it remarked on his "short and brilliant civic career," filled "with the intense turmoil of political partisanism." The paper spoke for the people of the county, who were "stricken with horror and regret at the manner of his taking off and deeply deplore it." Politics should be put aside "as we stand together in spirit by his grave, where he shall rest in peace and silently counsel us to peace, which was denied him living."

Captain Sam D. Willis, who had been the commander of the Greenville Company, 118th Infantry, Butler Guards, was selected by Governor Cooper to succeed Rector as sheriff out of several candidates who applied for the unexpired term. Willis's heroics during World War I were well known in the county, and he was famous for his command at the Hindenburg line in France. Born in 1891 to Confederate veteran G.C. Willis and Julia Hollis of Spartanburg, he married Ethel Gray of Georgia in 1915. Willis had

The funeral of Hendrix Rector. *Courtesy of the Greenville County Library.*

announced his intention to run for sheriff during the next election cycle and was the favorite to fill the abrupt vacancy.

Gosnell was arraigned on August 27, 1919, and he petitioned for a change of venue to federal court on the advice of his lawyers, Cothran, Dean & Cothran. Gosnell was convinced he could not get a fair trial in Greenville. He claimed self-defense, writing in his petition that Rector had made an "unprovoked and violent attack" on him with a pistol. Gosnell allegedly shot him as he was drawing his weapon. He claimed "necessary self-defense" in carrying out his duties as a deputy collector for the Internal Revenue Service. The state attorney's office, filed by Rector's family lawyers, J. Robert Martin of Bonham & Price and David Smoak, countered that the case should be remanded to the court of general sessions in Greenville County. They argued that Gosnell had "committed willful, premeditated and malicious murder," that he was not on any official duty for the Internal Revenue Service and that he had, in fact, spent most of the night with a known prostitute and was not in Greenville for work. There was no "just reason why Gosnell should not be tried in the state court." After a clash that lasted for several weeks, it was decided to try Gosnell in federal court, with J. William Thurmond taking the lead for the defense.

More motions were filed, resulting in a hearing in front of U.S. district judge H.H. Watkins. Watkins deemed the case should be tried in the court of general sessions back in Greenville. The trial finally began on May 11, 1920.

Sheriff Willis seemed to be settling into his position well and announced that he would run to remain sheriff in the next election. Carlos Rector was also mulling over a run as he continued to make a name for himself as a federal agent with the Internal Revenue Service, regularly capturing rumrunners and raiding stills.

Jake Gosnell's trial began with the state introducing three witnesses. Deputy Keller, who had been in Briscoe's Garage and ultimately arrested Gosnell, testified

Sam D. Willis. *Courtesy of the Greenville County Library.*

that when Rector had said "good morning" to Gosnell, tensions rose when the greeting was not returned. Gosnell told Rector that he didn't care to have any words with him. Keller stated that Rector then cursed Gosnell and made an "unmentionable reflection upon Gosnell's mother." Gosnell then rose from a kneeling posture at his car and began to fire at Rector. Dr. Black, who had performed the autopsy, took the stand to give his opinion that the bullet that hit Rector between his sixth and seventh ribs was the first shot. The state intended to prove that the shot was fired while Rector had his back partially turned to Gosnell. The third witness, Coroner J.H. Allison, told jurors that he, too, had been in the garage that day and was in the office with Rector and a small group, celebrating the Fourth of July holiday by drinking some "blockade beverages." He testified that Rector had one drink before leaving the office and heading into the garage. It was noted by Allison that Rector had taken the bottle and placed it in his pocket. The bottle was found on his person following the murder. Other witnesses were brought forward to support that Gosnell had made threats against Rector's life on various occasions. Star witness E.J. Doran, at twenty-seven-year veteran of the Charleston Police Department, told the court that he had been in Greenville that morning on his way to visit Caesars Head. He had not known the sheriff previously but called on him at the garage and was a part of the group that had a drink with him.

He stated that Rector was not "even slightly intoxicated." The defense countered first with its own surgeon, who brought the angle of the bullets into dispute, casting doubt as to whether Rector was turned away from Gosnell. The second day of the trial illuminated Rector's proclivity for drinking whiskey, including on the day he was killed. Witnesses testified that the sheriff imbibed frequently. The defense presented this as Rector being under the influence that morning and being the first to threaten Gosnell, thus supporting Gosnell's self-defense story and fulfilling his duty of being a federal agent. Jurors were shown X-rays and heard expert testimony to show the course of the bullets and where they came from. Anna Gosnell backed up her husband, stating that Rector's hand was going for his pistol. Gosnell himself testified that Rector had called him a demeaning name in front of his wife, and when he saw Rector move for his pistol, he reacted instantly to save his own life. After hearing from a total of eighty-five witnesses, Gosnell's fate was in the hands of the jury. The *State* newspaper of Columbia noted that the case was probably "the most voluminous of any in the history of criminal procedure in Greenville County." The jury considered the testimonies into the night, when the foreman told the court that they were irredeemably deadlocked, and the judge recessed them until the following day. The next day, it was clear the jurors could not come to an agreement, with eight men for acquittal and four for conviction, and a mistrial was ordered. Gosnell was out on a $4,000 bond.

Gosnell was back on the job, making the papers a month later for the capture of two youths and large quantities of "firewater." It was expected his second trial would begin during the court's October 1920 session.

The sheriff's office met the modern age in August 1920, when Willis swore in three motorcycle deputies. Speeding had become an epidemic, and the new cops were authorized to patrol the highways. The county expected to increase its income over $4,000 a month by writing out tickets for offenders at a minimum of $25 each. An advertisement appeared in the *Greenville News* on August 26, 1920, from Willis to "the voters of Greenville County"; he reminded them to vote for him in the upcoming election on August 31, stating that his duties as sheriff required him to be in court "every day next week," keeping him from spending "any time out in the county with the people," as he would like to. He wanted voters to know that if they didn't see him around, and that if that "is the sort of man you want for sheriff," they should cast their vote for him. Carlos Rector was running on the merits of his career, portraying himself as a "poor man" "belonging to that common herd," pointing out a lack of funds and influential people to back him. He said he was the man to bring experience and the one to "deliver the goods." He also promised that he would never employ "negro detectives" or commission "negro deputies." Rector accused Willis of giving a written permit to a negro named Charley White during the search for a fugitive, and putting his service front and center, he pointed out that Willis had been drafted. Rector was elected by the people to become sheriff in January, pressing Gosnell's attorney to ask for a speedy second trial, as Rector serving as sheriff might be prejudicial.

Carlos Rector. *Courtesy of the Greenville County Library.*

The press rolled out puff pieces, reminiscing about Hendrix and Carlos Rector being products of a log cabin from that "dismal section" known as Dark Corner. They described Carlos as a man who distilled "white lightning" as a teen, but he had become deeply religious twelve years prior and had given his heart to law enforcement. They quoted mama Rector as saying, "Not often does it fall to the lot of an old woman of the mountains to be the mother of two sheriffs of a great county like Greenville in the grand old state of South Carolina." It was noted that Carlos hoped to one day be elected to Congress, as his "late brother aspired."

As the Hugh Bramlett murder case was getting ready to tie up the court's time, Gosnell's second trial was put on the docket for 1921. This time, his lawyers were granted a change of venue, which the state did not object to, since the brother of the deceased was then Greenville County's sheriff. The trial was to take place in Pickens County. Solicitor David Smoak said that the proceedings would last about a week, and the cases on the Pickens docket were so numerous that the case could not be accommodated until September.

Hendrix Rector had been in the ground at Graceland Cemetery for over two years when the second Gosnell trial began on September 25, 1921. Several of the same witnesses came forward, and theatrics were utilized when Carlos Rector, acting as a model to portray his brother, stripped to his waist so that Dr. Black could show where the bullets had entered Hendrix's body. At the trial's close, the jury deliberated for over eleven hours. It was clear that a second mistrial was likely. Twenty-four hours later, the second mistrial was announced, and Gosnell was released from custody with a $5,000 bond. Solicitor Smoak promised that Gosnell would be tried again.

Since Gosnell had been a murder suspect for over two years, the Internal Revenue Service finally got around to dismissing him from federal service in December 1921. In February 1922, Gosnell and his wife leased the Old Hickory Inn in Pickens and became hotel proprietors. In July, he was back on the force after being tapped to join U.S. officers to enforce national Prohibition laws in Savannah, Georgia. There, he joined his cousin and former Hendrix Rector foe, Reuben.

The year 1922 appeared to be quiet for Rector, with his largest concern appearing to be public swimming pool safety and the prohibition of prize fights. He was also elected president of the South Carolina Association of Sheriffs. In December, he declared that the county had less "liquor here than in [a] half decade." When asked if he thought Greenville would have "complete Prohibition," Rector laughed and said, "If the people want it. The officer cannot make Prohibition alone. Just like every other law, it must have the sympathy of the people, and they must, at all times, be ready to cooperate with the officer in enforcing the laws."

Unidentified federal agents carrying confiscated liquor, 1921. *Courtesy of the Library of Congress.*

In 1923, it was wondered if Gosnell would ever face trial again. He was then a federal officer in New York City, doing some of the best work of his career, acting as a bodyguard of "Izzy" Einstein, a famous Prohibition sleuth. The stage had been set for trial number three to begin in February, and then an article was published in the February 14 edition of the *Pickens Sentinel* predicting an acquittal. On behalf of the state, attorney David Smoak claimed the article had "so warped and influenced public opinion" that a fair trial was not possible, and he filed a motion to charge the *Sentinel*'s editor Van Clayton with being in contempt of court. In addition to being the editor of the paper, Clayton was the county's superintendent of education. With Judge E.C. Dennis presiding, Clayton appeared before the court to prove he had not intended to influence the public. In a sworn affidavit, he explained that he was doing what he thought best, though he was inexperienced in the newspaper business and was unfamiliar with courtroom procedure. His lawyer highlighted his great works in Pickens as the county superintendent, focusing on how much he was helping the local youth. Judge Dennis fined Clayton ten dollars and didn't help matters much in his remarks, stating that it was an unfortunate thing "to bring a newspaper into court. They are wonderful influences for good and have been wonderful influences for law enforcement....It has been said that it is hard to convict a prominent white man of murder in South Carolina, regardless of the evidence, and that is true."

While Rector sought justice, Sam D. Willis, the sheriff who had succeeded Rector's brother after his death, announced that he would run again to oppose him. Jeff Gilreath even threw his hat in the ring, as did Cliff Bramlett and Ben Paris. Greenvillians were getting excited about the hotly contested "death match." The race came down to a runoff between Rector and Willis, resulting in a major victory for Willis. He received the badge on his coat from Rector on January 1, 1925.

A second blow hit the Rector family in October 1925, when Jake Gosnell was declared nol prossed (legal Latin that said the court was unwilling to pursue charges against him). Immediately, Carlos Rector, who was still an officer, swore out a warrant, charging him again for the murder of Hendrix Rector. Gosnell came to Greenville and turned himself in to Sheriff Willis, but he was immediately out again on bond. Rector swore that he would "fight to the bitter end" to see justice for his brother. "It was a heartless, cold-blooded affair, that man's killing my brother," Rector allegedly told Magistrate Cooley, who issued the warrant. "At least, that's what I think about it, and I don't propose to let the case die an unnatural death." Then, over six years after the murder of Hendrix Rector, Carlos petitioned the South Carolina attorney general John M. Daniel to take charge of Gosnell's case in early March 1926, as the solicitor's office didn't feel the case had sufficient evidence to be retried in Greenville. A.G. Daniel declined to interfere in the twice-tried case.

In July, it was reported that Gosnell had been fired on by a "band of unknown men" at a filling station that he owned with his wife in Pickens. In his account to the local police, Gosnell described an automobile arriving at the station around 10:00 p.m. He had closed the store for the night but lived approximately one hundred yards from the station. He alleged that two men stepped out from the vehicle; when he called out to them, they replied with buckshot. Gosnell returned fire, and when he found his pistol was empty, he retreated to his house. The men quickly got back in their car and fled the scene. He heard one of the men exclaim that he had been shot.

Sheriff Willis celebrated the end of 1926 by closing his 101st distillery. He had set a goal for himself to destroy 100 illegal stills and had surpassed his objective. He set a new target for 1927: to destroy 115 distilleries and capture at least two thousand gallons of liquor. He boasted that he would give a prize to the officer with the best record. In the spring, Governor John Richards called Willis out for turning a blind eye to golf being played on Sundays. In a strongly worded telegram followed up by a telephone call, he demanded that Willis follow the state "blue law," which prohibited sports on the Sabbath day. Willis wanted to consult with the attorney general, but the governor demanded that he had already given written orders to arrest any violators. The governor's campaign for rigid adherence also included regulations that banned the sale of soda water and general merchandise, other than pharmaceutical drugs, ice and milk. He ordered filling stations be closed as well. Willis again questioned the legality of these laws, announcing that he believed country clubs were private property. He wanted a legal interpretation. Willis and a state constable ended up arresting four men at the Greenville Country Club; one of the men mixed up in the fracas was attorney and former state senator Proctor Bonham. The men were released on their own recognizance and immediately motored to Asheville to pick up their game. This caused quite a stir with the citizens of Greenville, and they grew agitated with the strict mandates.

Rector had been made a state detective by Governor Richards and was based out of Columbia; meanwhile, his wife and children remained at their home in Greenville. The *Greenville News* often reported his exploits and family visits. It was noted that a country club in Aiken was granted an injunction, which it showed when Rector attempted to arrest some Sunday golfers there. The governor appeared to be using Rector to enforce the Sabbath observance that Willis was lenient on.

On June 11, 1927, Sheriff Willis was returning to his home at 219 East Stone Avenue around midnight, when he was shot four times in his garage as he got out of his car. The first investigators on site found a crime scene with Willis laying in the doorway; one bullet had passed through his forehead, and another was in his heart. The driver's-side door of his car was open with the keys inside, prompting the detectives to consider that Willis had seen someone in the garage and exited his vehicle abruptly. His pistol was still holstered. Neighbors heard the shots and reported seeing a "negro in shirt sleeves enter the sidewalk near the sheriff's home." Others claimed they saw the man running. Willis's wife, Ethel, told police that after she heard the shots, she had also seen the man as he ran by the window. Almost eight years to the day after the murder of Hendrix Rector, another popular sheriff was dead.

The next day, thousands of sorrowful residents poured in and out of the Willises' home through much of the afternoon. Willis's widow and four young daughters received floral arrangements, phone messages and telegrams expressing sympathy from all over the state. Twenty-five knights of the Ku Klux Klan even appeared in full regalia to lay a robe and cross of the order on the casket, disappearing as silently as they had arrived. Governor Richards called out the militia and the Butler Guards, Willis's former unit, to keep the peace and prevent any disorder. John Parks, the county coroner, was sworn in as the acting sheriff while Richards began to think of successors. A heavy veil of sadness hung over the city once again.

The first theory that officers worked was that the killing had been orchestrated by a liquor ring. A tip that an unnamed man had warned Willis several days prior that he would be shot led investigators to believe that the murder had been well-thought-out, and they began to look at a "negro gun for hire" scenario. Willis's great devastation of bootlegging circles gave credence to this hypothesis. Richards dispatched several state officers, including Carlos Rector, to work the high-profile case, asking them to remain until the mystery was solved. These officers investigated clues that a white man was the assassin, citing that it was the darkness of the night that made it difficult for the person who was seen running to have been seen clearly by the eyewitnesses.

As the nation celebrated the return of Charles Lindbergh and the *Spirit of St. Louis* to New York, Sheriff Willis was laid to rest in Springwood Cemetery in a gray casket with a plate bearing the inscription "Daddy." His widow wore a heavy veil and was accompanied by two men, her brother-in-law and Deputy Sheriff Henry Townsend, a close friend of the slain officer. It was opined by Willis's elderly mother that three of his daughters were so young, they may not remember their father as they grew up, save for Virginia, who was eleven years old. The closed courthouse was adorned in black crepe and lowered its flag to half-mast. Virtually all who were able from Willis's force were in attendance, as were officers from nearby communities. Reminiscent of the funeral for Hendrix Rector, throngs filled the church and the surrounding streets, as well as the graveside for the service.

After the funeral, a new theory emerged in the investigation, and the police arrested Deputy Sheriff Henry Townsend. They kept him "under heavy guard" at the state penitentiary in Columbia. Townsend and Willis had been friends for years and fought side by side in France during the war. He had acted as Willis's deputy since the day he took office. Townsend's arrest at the home of Willis's widow fueled rumors of a possible love triangle, and Greenville was soon invested in the scandal.

On June 16, 1927, Richards named Carlos Rector as Willis's successor. "After mature deliberation" between strong candidates, including Rector, C.R. Bramlett and Riley Rowley, Richards chose Rector for "his good record as sheriff" and "his splendid work as a state constable and detective." Rector issued a statement to say that he would lend his "strength and energy as sheriff to bring the guilty person or persons" responsible for the murder of Willis "to justice."

Officers advanced a theory of a so-called eternal triangle. They believed that Townsend and Ethel Willis had been surprised by the arrival of the sheriff on that fateful night and that Townsend then "shot his way out." Hedda Hopper, the famed gossip columnist of Hollywood's golden heyday, could not have concocted a more salacious tale. Mrs. Willis was also jailed, and both she and Townsend were dragged through the mud in the press. Morbid curiosity led many to drive by the jailhouse, hoping for a glimpse of the black widow. Affidavits were presented to prove the intimate entanglement, as a roomer in the Willises' home described that Townsend and his wife had come to the house much later after the shooting, probably around 4:00 a.m. Mrs. Townsend came and went. She stated that later that morning, Mrs. Willis and Mr. Townsend were sitting on the bed, talking at a very low volume and holding hands. She often saw them hold hands. Deputy Bramlett also swore in an affidavit that he had frequently seen the pair together for the last eighteen months. It was not uncommon for Mrs.

Willis to come to the office and pick Townsend up in her car when Sheriff Willis was not around. He also declared that he and Townsend had been on a call together in the last two weeks and that Townsend had talked about relations with a married woman that he was going to "cut out." The state presented evidence of finding a woman's footprint pointing toward the spot where Willis had fallen and another track to the rear of Mrs. Willis's car. They also found a man's footprints and some spent shells. It was shown that a print was taken of Mrs. Willis's shoes and that they matched, but those tracks could have been made at any time, especially after Mrs. Willis heard the shots and went to check on her husband. Sheriff Willis's sister Rosa Goodwin testified that her brother and Henry Townsend were as close as brothers and that the entire family had the "utmost confidence in the innocence of Mrs. Ethel Willis and believes that charges against her are absolutely false and without foundation." Townsend's lawyers dropped a bombshell when it was revealed that Townsend had a hernia operation on June 9 and had been in the hospital until the day of the shooting. According to the doctor, Townsend was resting in bed the evening Willis was slain and he would have been physically unable to stand around in a garage—much less run away. The state's case fell apart, and both Ethel Willis and Henry Townsend were acquitted. They each filed suits against the *Greenville News* to the tune of $50,000 apiece, as they claimed that what the newspaper had published was "defamatory and injurious" to their reputations. The paper defended itself, saying that it was merely doing its job and reporting on what the cops said and what was presented in court. It claimed it was not only the paper's "privilege, but its duty to make publication of the facts." Willis's murder case went back to the unsolved desk.

In 1928, Cliff Bramlett ran against Rector for sheriff, claiming that Rector was using cases attributed to Willis and touting them as his own record. Rector flatly denied this, and they argued back and forth in the papers. When Bramlett ultimately defeated the incumbent, he vowed to continue the search for Willis's killer. Also notable in this election was that the first woman in the South Carolina General Assembly was seated when Mary Ellis won the state senate seat for Jasper County. Modernization continued when the sheriff-elect announced that he would institute all-night patrols and requested ten additional deputies to do so.

The Willis case had been cold for two years when a Black man named Blair Rook turned himself in to Bramlett's department on a warm August day in 1929. Rook volunteered to officers that he had been "haunted by the memory of the dead sheriff." He said that he had been made a promise of

$500 by two white men to perpetrate the act but only received $50 of what had been promised. Bramlett had him write out a confession, in which he told the story of the night's events in great detail, describing that he and one of the white men had driven past Willis's house several times when the garage where Willis would enter with his car was pointed out to him. They left and got some liquor, and Rook felt "pretty good." He waited in some bushes outside the garage for at least an hour. "Then I saw a car come in and got up. When the automobile came into the garage, I walked to the corner. When the sheriff came out and started to the house, I stepped out. He heard me and turned around. I did not see him reach for a gun. I just shot without speaking. He never spoke neither. I saw him stagger and stepped closer. I shot two more times and saw him start to fall. Then I turned around and walked down the driveway."

The first of these two accomplices to be named was Harmon Moore, a deputy sheriff who had served under Rector. Moore claimed that everything Blair Rook had to say was a lie. Rook was brought into the room to confront Moore and fingered him as the man who had driven him in front of Willis's home. Moore told the officers he had not been in town on the night Willis was killed. A few lawyers in the city tried to say that Rook was a crackpot, but Bramlett felt his story was credible, and people who knew the thirty-one-year-old described him as being "in possession of all his faculties." In November, Rook led investigators to the pistol used in the crime. He said he had thrown it in a briar patch in the upper part of the county, and it was right where he said it would be.

The walls must have been closing in on the second suspect, but Bramlett was keeping that name close to his chest. Perhaps he was waiting to see what this individual would say or do while he gathered more evidence. And when he interfered in the Harmon case, helping cause a mistrial in January 1930, the name of the second conspirator was finally revealed to be none other than Carlos Rector. Carlos Rector, the puritanical two-time sheriff of Greenville who had stood by while Willis's best friend and widow had been put on trial for the world to see in the alleged "eternal triangle," had approached the wife of the jury foreman and told her that Rook had gone back on his testimony and that the prosecutors would have to "get him shaped up again." Carlos Rector, whose own brother had been slain in 1919, had orchestrated the offing of the sitting sheriff, allegedly because Willis was, in his mind, the "only man in Greenville County who can beat me for sheriff."

At the trial in December 1930, Rector was tried alongside Harmon, who was being retried. The state brought forth four other men, who stated that they had either been approached by Rector to do the killing or were aware of the plot on Willis. A Black man named Ed Cuffie testified that he had been approached by Rector and a woman identified only as "Miss Cook" multiple times. From the stand, he stated that Miss Cook had presented him with a pocketbook full of money to slay Willis. He claimed Rector had brought him a shotgun and shells, but he had refused them. Miss Cook was never identified during the proceedings, but it was revealed that the plot had been hatched in 1924, around the time Rector had been defeated by Willis. The newly married Ethel Willis Medlock took the stand to recount her actions that night after she found her husband. She testified that she "knew about the enmity between her husband and Rector" and had even gone to the governor at the time, asking to be appointed interim sheriff herself so that she could "check up Sam's books and straighten his affairs before Carlos could get in the office." On December 10, the jurors rendered a guilty verdict for both men; Rook's trial had not started yet. Rector and Harmon were sentenced to ten years' hard labor. It seemed some justice might prevail.

Rector assembled a strong defense team that included Cole Blease, the former governor and U.S. senator who had once been a political ally of his brother. Rector ran his coffers dry with appeals and psychological assessments on Rook. The reports consistently found Rook sane. The supreme court ultimately upheld the convictions for Rector and Moore, and they began their sentences in 1932.

Blair Rook was sentenced to life in prison and was paroled after twenty-three years in 1955.

Carlos Rector served six years before being paroled by Governor Olin Johnston in 1938. He was pardoned in 1939, after which, he returned to Greenville and ran for sheriff in 1940, but he was overwhelmingly defeated. He lived until the ripe old age of eighty-two, dying in 1966.

Harmon Moore was paroled in July 1936 by Governor Johnston.

Jake Gosnell retired from federal service in 1933 and was never tried again for the murder of Hendrix Rector. He ran a Texaco Filling Station on Pickens-Easley Highway until his death of a cerebral hemorrhage in 1943. He was seventy-one years old.

Evie Rector, Hendrix's widow, was remarried in 1921 to Hendrix and Carlos's brother, decorated war hero Jefferson McCrary Rector. They lived in the same home off Laurens Road that had been occupied by her and Hendrix. She died in 1947. Jefferson would follow several years later, in 1961. They were all buried in the family plot at Graceland Cemetery.

ACCIDENTAL ENDS

The early twentieth century brought huge mills to Greenville, and with them, a new labor opportunity arose. Men and women from the Appalachians and bordering states moved their entire households. Mill communities became cities unto themselves, with schools, general mercantile stores, groceries and doctors. Larger mills offered credit systems, in which items were deducted from future paychecks, and some had their own currency in the form of vouchers or "looneys." The majority of workers had been farming laborers and were briefly trained or self-taught on how to handle large machinery without safety protocols. Dismemberment, disease and deafness were unfortunate side effects of mill life.

An accident in 1903 claimed the life of Alfred Ervin Waldrop. He was working in a gristmill with the task of making a repair. As he placed a belt on the pulley of the machine, he became entangled in the mechanism. One arm was severed at the shoulder as he went over the wheel for several turns. It took witnesses several minutes to extract him. He bled out rapidly and died on the spot, leaving behind a wife and three small children.

Children were not spared from mill work, and many started as young as six years old, attending school and then working after school into the early evening. It was not rare for one mom to care for many of the children in the close-knit community while their parents worked.

A twelve-year-old girl named Avie Lee Smith was at a neighbor's home in Brandon Mill in May 1917 when she was struck by lightning. The jolt entered her body from a light socket she was standing under, instantly killing her and tearing up the floor beneath her. Other occupants were spared, but the act of God put a heavy gloom over the Brandon residents. She was buried in a section of Graceland Cemetery that was then known as the "Brandon Cemetery."

The "Great Migration" of the early 1900s and people making steady pay increased interest in automobile ownership. When Ford invented the affordable Model T, cars were no longer a toy for the elite. These machines soon became a menacing problem on the South Carolina roads throughout the country. The city did not have speed limits or stop signs until 1909. The *Greenville News* regularly espoused reckless driving and called for stricter laws and enforcement. Accidents claimed the lives of many locals.

Decades after the influx of cars into the area, one of Greenville's most bizarre accidents occurred on September 19, 1941. Police were in pursuit of a young white male in a stolen car when the car crashed into a house and

Left: Alfred Ervin Waldrop. *Courtesy of Ray Waldrop.*

Below: Remnants of Berry Mill on Highway 14. *Photograph by John Stoy.*

A crashed automobile on North Main Street and Park Avenue, 1912. *Courtesy of the Greenville County Library.*

burst into flames. The victim became enveloped in an inferno. The charred husk of human remains made identification impossible. Authorities and the papers put out calls for assistance in uncovering the man's identity, but his name remained a mystery. Hundreds of people filed into McAfee Funeral Home in hopes of recognizing the cremated corpse, but no one claimed him. Woodlawn Memorial Park donated a plot for the burial, where he remains today, not far from the bell tower under a memorial that reads "Unidentified Man—died September 19, 1941, buried September 21, 1941."

THE RIDE TO LIBERTY

In Archie Huff's seminal history *Greenville: The History of the City and County in the South Carolina Piedmont*, he wrote:

> *In the city of Greenville, blacks lived on almost every street and in every section. Black-owned businesses were quite common—dominating the hacking and drayage business, as well as bakeries, blacksmith shops, and*

catering. As late as 1899, there were six black-owned barbershops on Main Street, with fifteen barbers, three retail stores, one meat market, and three restaurants.

He also notes that in the late 1800s, "the mood of the nation, as well as the South, had begun to change." By 1882, Democrats were firmly in control of South Carolina and did not want a Republican revival in the state. A majority of the Black community voted Republican. To remove this threat, the general assembly passed the "Eight Box Law," a literacy test that separated boxes for ballots of each designated office. A voter would need to select the correct box to put their ballot in, or it would not count. Many ballots were rejected, disenfranchising a great number of Black voters. A mindset centered on segregation took hold, and laws were passed separating white and Black students in schools. This soon bled over to rules for railroad cars, trolleys and the workplace.

The Klan reared its pointy head in the district in the 1920s. A parade was held in 1926, and Klansmen marched through a Black business area downtown like deranged wizards, conducting their signature cross burning and causing fear and terror in the community. Like a leaky gasoline can next to an open flame, something was bound to eventually blow.

On November 16, 1933, "a white-robed body of men, masked and hooded," barged through the door at the home of George Green and his wife, Mary, in Taylors. Green, a tenant farmer for C.F. James, had been involved in a dispute with his landlord, and James wanted him gone. Mary testified that when they did not move out soon enough, James enlisted the help of a mob to scare and murder her husband. He was shot in the home and died in her arms. The magistrate for Taylors, J.H. Wood, testified that he had known "old George" for some time and knew of the trouble between Green and James. But he also knew that, by law, Green was allowed to remain in the home until the end of the year. A Mr. Monk of Taylors attested that he had delivered a message to the Klan on behalf of James "with reference to Green's being moved out of the house." A total of seventeen men were charged with lynching George Green, including James, but none was convicted.

Greenville's most heinous act took place after Valentine's Day in 1947, when Yellow Cab driver Thomas Brown picked up a fare on Markley and Calhoun Streets. Brown had been hired by a young Black man for a ride to Liberty. The trip resulted in Brown being found on the ground near his wrecked cab, bleeding from three stab wounds. He had suffered a tremendous beating. En route to the hospital, Brown gave a description of his attacker: a "large, black negro."

Pickens deputies alleged they had followed footprints (over a mile) from the cab to the home of Willie Earle's mother, Tessie. Earle (twenty-four) suffered from epilepsy and was prone to seizures, making it hard for him to maintain consistent employment. As of late, this had caused depression for the young man, who liked to drown his sorrows in alcohol. He had been out drinking with friends the night he called a cab. In the home, the deputies found what they assumed was money taken from Brown as well as a "bloodstained" jacket and shoes that bore the prints they had followed there. Earle was not in the home at the time of the search but was arrested the next day, never making any attempt to flee. A knife with dried blood had been found on him, but no blood type evidence was taken from it. Earle denied that he had ever been in Brown's cab.

With Brown on his deathbed, a group of taxi drivers from multiple companies were rounded up by Roosevelt Herd, who acted as a ringleader. In a café at the back of the courthouse, in the shadow of the sheriff's office, a plot was hatched to organize the men, caravan to the Pickens Jail and capture the man who had wronged one of their own. There had been, on the record, several instances of assault and robbery on taxi drivers who roamed throughout the city at all hours on any given night. When little was done, and few arrests were made, the cabbies became resentful toward the police. Combined with the fact that justice in Greenville could be compared to holding water in your hand, the drivers had little confidence that something would be remedied. Once assembled, the procession of taxis converged on the secluded Pickens Jail under cover of night. The indignant mob confronted jailer Ed Gilstrap and demanded that he turn over "the negro." Gilstrap, fearing for his own safety and that of his family, who lived on the premises, surrendered Earle to the gang.

Webster's Dictionary describes *mob mentality* as "a large and disorderly crowd of people, especially one bent on riotous or destructive action," and that's just what these men were when they stole Willie Earle from jail and drove him to a secluded part of Bramlett Road. Someone suggested they carry him to the hospital so Brown could identify him. Earle was not even the confirmed killer, but that mattered little to the enraged men who, at that point, merely saw him as a symbol of their rage and commenced with the beating. Later statements described "the tearing of cloth and flesh." As Earle cried out, "Lord, you done killed me," the horde, frenzied like coyotes, cut his throat from ear to ear, exposing his windpipe, and then

Old Pickens Jail. *Photograph by John Stoy.*

gouged out his eyes before Herd finished him with a final shotgun blast. Afterward, someone telephoned a Black funeral home, and the coroner discovered Earle's mutilated remains. Thomas Brown was also dead, having passed away from his injuries in St. Francis Hospital.

Thirty-six long hours ticked by before Attorney General Tom Clark sent agents from the FBI to investigate and apprehend the Earle murderers. This apparently took the men by surprise, as lynching was regarded as dueling had been in the past—it was practically a right. Law enforcement usually looked the other way in such instances. Newly appointed governor Strom Thurmond threw his immediate support behind the bureau. In total, thirty-one men, mostly taxi drivers, were arrested and put on trial.

The "Black press" were the only papers that covered Earle's funeral. Tessie Earle's pastor and the funeral home pulled together to cover the expenses, and Willie Earle was laid to rest near his father, Richard, at the Abel Church in Clemson.

The "trial of the century" began on a sweltering day in May. The courtroom was filled with the defendants, described by British writer Rebecca West, who covered the trial for the *New Yorker*, in "Opera in Greenville" as "tough guys, untainted by intellectualism." The men were accompanied to court by their families. About 200 white Greenville citizens, divided over the entire affair, filled chairs behind the proceedings, while approximately 150 Black citizens filled the upper gallery, along with writers from the Black newspapers, who were also relegated to the balcony. A press table downstairs, full of local and national reporters, was in front of the court. The 12 white male jurors were mostly mill workers, and they included salesmen, a mechanic and a farmer. Robert T. Ashmore and Sam Watt served as prosecutors, while local defense attorney Thomas Wofford, Ben Bolt and John Bolt Culbertson headed up the defense. Family members and spectators alike recoiled as statements were read aloud in court, explaining what the men had done to Earle.

Ashmore and Watt made the best of what evidence they had, which mostly consisted of the statements that had been taken by the FBI before the men were or even thought they would be arrested. The statements had not been sworn to. Watt vehemently portrayed lynching as a vile evil that was to be reviled by a God-fearing people.

For the defense, Culbertson addressed the jury with a speech that West depicted as "untainted by any regard for the values of civilization." She noted Culbertson's "reputation in the South as a liberal" and a supposed "friend to the emancipation of the negroes" while referring to "hypocrisy, based on a profound contempt for his fellow men." His defense of the "good ol' boys" played right into the hands of those who believed they had been justified in their actions. He also insinuated that the FBI had been sent in to obtain a lynching conviction to overturn Democratic seats and that this was nothing more than political folly.

Like Atticus Finch defending Tom Robinson in *To Kill a Mockingbird*, it was not looking good in this southern courtroom for justice for Willie Earle, but while the jury deliberated, the outcome was still unclear. The defendants and their families looked sullen and scared. West wrote that the "place was given up to gloom." When the attorneys returned to their seats and the judge called for order in the court, his face turned ruddy as he read the verdict to himself, and as the clerk read the outcome to the courtroom, he left without a word. The thirty-one had been acquitted. The courtroom erupted in cheers, and a party-like atmosphere soon took hold as other spectators filed out silently. Culbertson dashed about the room like he had won a gold medal.

It was never proven that Wille Earle committed the murder of Thomas Brown. Earle had been held previously on minor charges. One arrest in Greenville in 1946 for property damage while intoxicated produced a mugshot

Willie Earle, 1946 mugshot. *Courtesy of the Greenville Police Department.*

but little else in proving that he might have been capable of murder. Brown had described his attacker as "large," yet Earle stood at only five feet, nine inches tall. His mother admitted that he had regular "spells," referring to his epilepsy, and some who knew him described him as "slow." After his arrest, it had been asserted in the papers that she had been interviewed by police, but Tessie remained steadfast that she had never spoken to authorities or was asked to identify "anything to anybody." She stated that Earle had taken a bus to Liberty that night, not a cab. Police reports that allege Brown had picked up "two intoxicated negro men" that fateful night have mysteriously vanished. Cab records and court testimonies have been lost or destroyed, fueling a conspiracy. It is likely that Brown's true killer got away with murder.

Famed reporter and radioman Walter Winchell, the Rush Limbaugh of his day who helped thrust this story into the national spotlight, took to the airwaves on ABC to declare that the verdict was "a great triumph indeed for Mr. Hitler." He went on to say that "your country is embarrassed by you before the other nations of the world."

Tessie Earle, amid her grief, wanted to keep the thought and name of her son in the public sphere. Unfortunately, she ended up a pawn for activists, as described in the book *They Stole Him Out of Jail* by William B. Gravely:

> *Her dilemma came from competing agendas of activists who wanted to shape her into their versions of the symbolic black mother of a lynching*

victim. Tessie Earle was not prepared for the city's unfamiliar black, liberal, socialist and Marxist political scene.

The ongoing problems of misattribution and public relations efforts to have her promote different agendas shadowed her extended stay.… These hustlers were turning her presence into a hoax.

Tessie eventually cut ties with those who were trying to use her for their own agendas.

The vile outcome of Willie Earle's lynching and subsequent trial presented a great paradox to the old South, a pattern of injustice stemming back to the city's inception versus religious, conservative-leaning beliefs in right and wrong. Willie Earle became the last person lynched in South Carolina, his case spurring an antilynching movement and laying the groundwork for future civil rights activism. West concluded that "wickedness itself had been aware of the slowing of its pulse. The will of the South had made its decision." Defense attorney Culbertson later had a change of heart, drawing from the shame of his actions, and became a champion for integration, traveling throughout the state for the South Carolina NAACP. In 1958, he assisted Tessie Earle in finally settling Willie Earle's estate in probate court after she had waited a decade.

A drive through Liberty today shows a town virtually unchanged since 1947, with many of the old buildings that Tessie Earle knew well. Her home on Palmetto Street is no longer there, but the street itself can almost be found by accident, as it is right off Main Street. Willie Earle's story is not hidden in Greenville; over the years, there have been numerous symposiums and events for "public recollection." One historical marker behind the Greenville Courthouse marks the site of the trial. Another, once marking the site of the mob killing on Bramlett Road, now sits near Earle's grave after it was repeatedly vandalized. This case remains a controversy and stirs strong emotion, even now.

When Martin Luther King Jr. gave his "I Have a Dream" speech in 1963, he evoked the scripture of Amos when he said, "We will not be satisfied until justice rolls down like the water and righteousness like a mighty stream." Like the flow of the Reedy River, humanity continues to pursue what is just and un-wicked.

BIBLIOGRAPHY

Archives and Manuscripts

Abbeville Press and Banner (Abbeville, SC). "Revenue Detective Rufus Springs Shot and Killed." April 24, 1878. www.newspapers.com.

Abstracts of General Sessions Court Case Rolls. Washington District, South Carolina, 1792–99. Greenville County, South Carolina, 1787–99.

Ancestry. "1850 United States Census, Christ Church Parish, Charleston, South Carolina, entry for Saml W. Bates." www.ancestry.com.

———. "1830 United States Census, Charleston, South Carolina, entry for Saml W. Bates." www.ancestry.com.

———. "1940 United States Census, Charlotte, Mecklenburg, North Carolina, entry for Cora M. Bramlett." www.ancestry.com.

———. "1930 United States Census, Seneca, Oconee, South Carolina, entry for Hugh Bramlet." www.ancestry.com.

———. "South Carolina, U.S. Wills and Probate Records, 1670–1980, entry for Elijah Pike, Sr." www.ancestry.com.

Bloody Bill Bates Archive File. Greenville County Library, South Carolina Room.

Casetext. "*Green v. Greenville County*, Supreme Court of South Carolina, June 11, 1935." www.casetext.com.

———. "*The State v. Bramlett*, Supreme Court of South Carolina, 26 July 1920." www.casetext.com.

Find a Grave. "Online Memorial, entry for Alfred Ervin Waldrop, Died 6 July 1903." www.findagrave.com.

———. "Online Memorial, entry for Avie Lee Smith, Died 22 May 1917." www.findagrave.com.

———. "Online Memorial, entry for John Dill, Died 11 February 1938." www.findagrave.com.

Gaffney Ledger (Gaffney, SC). "Alex Pitman Returns to Beloved Mountain." April 8, 1930. www.newspapers.com.

———. "Eight Years' Service, Father and Son Free." October 10, 1930. www.newspapers.com.

———. "Father and Son to Die for Death of Constable." May 24, 1924.

———. "Governor Not Likely to Release Pittman." December 22, 1927. www.newspapers.com.

———. "Verdict of Guilty for Two Pittman's." May 20, 1924. www.newspapers.com.

Greenville County Coroner's Inquisition Files, South Carolina Department of Archives & History, Columbia, SC. "The State vs. The Dead Body of Allen, 4 September 1858." www.CSIDixie.org.

———. "The State vs. The Dead Body of Elijah Pike, 28 December 1856." www.CSIDixie.org.

———. "The State vs. The Dead Body of Mose, 28 August 1851." www.CSIDixie.org.

———. "The State vs. The Dead Body of Negro Slave Woman, 12 July 1851." www.CSIDixie.org.

———. "The State vs. The Dead Body of Rufus Springs, 20 April 1878." www.CSIDixie.org.

———. "The State vs. The Dead Body of Samuel Bates, 9 July 1851." www.CSIDixie.org.

Greenville News, 1881–1958. www.newspapers.com and South Carolina Room, Greenville Public Library.

Howard, Clarence G. "Driver for Agents Badly Wounded by Bootlegger Suspect." *Florence Morning News* (Florence, SC), April 22, 1930. www.newspapers.com.

Kirby, J.D. "A Detailed Report of the Unfortunate Affair." *Gaffney Ledger* (Gaffney, SC), March 19, 1896. www.newspapers.com.

Maxwell, Robert. "Columbia, Nov. 21." *Hartford Courant* (Hartford, CT), December 18, 1797. www.newspapers.com.

People's Journal (Pickens, SC). "The Celebrated Perry-Bynum Duel." July 8, 1897. www.newspapers.com.

Prince, John. "Found Dead." *Greenville Enterprise* (Greenville, SC), July 17, 1856. www.newspapers.com.

Sacramento Daily Union (Sacramento, CA). "Perry–Bynum Duel." October 18, 1897. California Digital Newspaper Collection, University of California–Riverside.

Southern, Gipson. "Melancholy Occurrence." *Greenville Enterprise* (Greenville, SC), February 28, 1856. www.newspapers.com.

Southern Historical Collection, North Carolina Library. The Benjamin Franklin Perry Papers. Microfilm, Greenville County Library, South Carolina Room.

Times and Democrat (Orangeburg, SC). "South Carolina Mountain Romance Culminates with Wedding in Jail." November 7, 1925. www.newspapers.com.

University of South Carolina, South Caroliniana Library. Affidavit, sworn by Richard Pearis, November 11, 1775.

———. Letter, William Henry Drayton to Richard Pearis, November 8, 1775.

———. Robert Gouedy deposition, 1775 July 10.

Ward, Jackson. "The Revenue Persecution." *News and Herald* (Winnsboro, SC), February 17, 1877. www.newspapers.com.

Watchman and Southron (Sumter, SC). "McLeod Blames Conditions of Pittman's on Society." February 3, 1926. www.newspapers.com.

———. "Wife of Holland Pittman Assumes Responsibility for Crime Which Her Husband Was Convicted and Sentenced to Death." January 30, 1926. www.newspapers.com.

Media

Ninety Six National Historic Site. "Clash of the Commanders IV: Richard Pearis." Video. www.youtube.com.

SuckerPunchPictures. "The Outlaw Lewis Redmond." Video, September 6, 2016. www.youtube.com.

Online Sources

Kneeland, Linda Kay. "African American Suffering and Suicide Under Slavery." Scholar Works, Montana State University. www.scholarworks.montana.edu.

McHugh/Paris Genealogy. www.donmchugh.tripod.com.
SCETV. "Memories of a Mill Town." www.digital.scetv.org.

Published Works

Batson, Mann. *A History of the Upper Part of Greenville County, South Carolina.* Greenville, SC: Faith Printing Co., 1993.

Campbell, Dean. *The Rest of Dark Corner's Twice-Told Tales.* Landrum, SC: Tamaczar Productions, 2017.

———. *Twice-Told Tales of the Dark Corner.* Landrum, SC: Tamaczar Productions, 2013.

Duncan, Barbara R. "Going to Water: A Cherokee Ritual in Its Contemporary Context." *Journal of the Appalachian Studies Association* 5 (1993): 94–99.

Gilreath, John H. *P.D. Gilreath High Sheriff.* Greenville, SC: John H. Gilreath, 1968.

Gregory, James V., and James Walton Lawrence Sr. *Indians, Bloodshed, Tears, Churches, & Schools; It All Started at Fort Gowen.* Kearney, NE: Morris Publishing, 2003.

Helsley, Alexia Jones. *Hidden History of Greenville County.* Charleston, SC: The History Press, 2009.

Howard, James A. *Dark Corner Heritage.* 1980. Reprint, Gowensville, SC: Greater Gowensville Association, 2006.

Howe, George. *History of the Presbyterian Church.* Columbia, SC: Duffie & Chapman, 1870. www.books.google.com.

Huff, Archie Vernon, Jr. *Greenville: The History of the City and County in the South Carolina Piedmont.* Columbia: University of South Carolina Press, 1995.

Klein, Rachel N. "Ordering the Backcountry: The South Carolina Regulation." *William and Mary Quarterly* 38, no. 4 (1981): 661–80. doi:10.2307/1918909.

Landrum, J.B.O. *Colonial Revolutionary History of Upper South Carolina.* 1897. Reprint, London: Forgotten Books, 2015.

Lee, Harper. *To Kill a Mockingbird.* New York: HarperCollins, 1960.

Long, J. Grahame. *Dueling in Charleston: Violence Refined in the Holy City.* Charleston, SC: The History Press, 2012.

McNeely, Patricia. "Dueling Editors—The Nullification Plot of 1832." In *Words at War: The Civil War and American Journalism.* West Lafayette, IN: Purdue University Press, 2008.

Moore, John Hammond. *Carnival of Blood: Dueling, Lynching, and Murder in South Carolina 1880–1920*. Columbia: University of South Carolina Press, 2006.

Piecuch, Jim. "Richard Pearis and the Mobilization of South Carolina's Backcountry Loyalists." *Journal of the American Revolution* (2014): n.p.

Sawyer, Richard. *10,000 Years of Greenville County, South Carolina History*. Greenville, SC: Greenville County Historical Society, 1997.

Smith, Roy McBee. *Vardry McBee: Man of Reason in an Age of Extremes*. Greenville, SC: Laurel Heritage Press, 1992.

Stewart, Bruce E. *King of the Moonshiners*. Knoxville: University of Tennessee Press, 2008.

Walther, Eric H. *William Lowndes Yancey and the Coming of the Civil War*. Chapel Hill: University of North Carolina Press, 2006.

West, Rebecca. "Opera in Greenville." *New Yorker*, June 6, 1947.

White, J. Warren, MD. *Paris Mountain*. Greenville, SC: South Carolina Collection, South Carolina Room, Greenville Public Library, 1945.

ABOUT THE AUTHOR

*J*ennifer Stoy is a professional genealogist and the creator of "Weird Genealogy Minute" videos on YouTube. She was previously employed in the entertainment industry as an extras' casting director and then worked ten years in the South Carolina funeral business. She lives in Greenville, South Carolina, with her husband, daughter and assorted pets.

For more information about Jennifer, visit:
www.weirdgenealogy.com